MW01127801

The Nondual Universe

The Spirituality of Enlightenment Made Simple for the Western Mind

by

James F. Twyman

Online Video Lessons For The Nondual Universe

If you would like to get the most out of this book, access the video lessons James Twyman recorded to accompany all 54 lessons. Each one is short, concise, and gives a deeper glimpse into the actual experience of enlightenment. Simply go to http://worldpeacepulse.com/nonduallessons.

Books by James F. Twyman

The Moses Code

The Art of Spiritual Peacemaking

The Barn Dance

Emissary of Light

Emissary of Love

Giovanni and the Camino of St. Francis

I AM Wishes Fulfilled Meditation
(with Dr. Wayne Dyer)

The Kabbalah Code: A True Adventure
(with Philip Gruber)

Love, God, and the Art of French Cooking

Messages From Thomas

The Prayer of St. Francis

Praying Peace

The Proof
(with Anakha Coman)

The Proposing Tree

St. Francis and the Animals Who Loved Him

The Secret of the Beloved Disciple

Ten Spiritual Lessons I Learned at the Mall

Touching the Divine

The Impersonal Light: Journey into I AM Consciousness

The Remembrance Of God 51

The Distant Horizon..54

The Unreal Shadow...57

The Echo Chamber 60

The One...62

God's Fool..64

An Unwavering Desire 67

Are You Ready To Give Everything?....................................70

That Which Seems To Die 72

All-Encompassing Love...76

Everywhere At Every Moment 80

Allow It To Be Done 84

True Power...87

Everything..90

A Single Goal...92

Eyes That See And Ears That Hear......................................95

The State Of Perfect Non-Being 98

The Solution Of the Soul 101

Understanding Level Confusion 103

You Returning To You..107

The Illusion Of "i" 111

The Key Attachment Of The Split-Mind 114

Liberation from Separate-Self...118

Why Not Now? 121

The Moment You Have Been Waiting For............................124

There Is Nothing In This World That Can Contain You 126

You Were Made For And By Love...129

God's Love Has Never Been Compromised...........................132

There Is Nothing Left To Say 135

You Can Not Hide Forever 137

The Moment Of Your Awakening..140

God's Point Of View..143

The Cornerstone Of God's Creation 146

The World You Seem To See 149

Which Would You Choose: A Shield Or A Sword? 151

The Uncomfortable Path To God...153

In Conclusion 155

Acknowledgments

Eternal gratitude to Baraka who continues to be Truly Helpful, my favorite teaching partner Vicki Poppe, all my brothers and sisters at Namaste Village, and Chuck Anderson, my Great Awakener.

Nondual Versus Dual

You will never intellectually understand what you are about to read, but something remarkable will happen if you give up the need to "figure out" the Truth you will find in this book — you will discover that the Truth found in this book figured you out a very long time ago. Can you imagine anything better? Actually, you can not, and that is the point. You are about to enter into an experience unlike anything you have ever known before, yet the most intimate you will ever enjoy.

What does that mean exactly? Once again, it is impossible to explain with words since the experience this book points to exists beyond the limitation of symbols, which is what words are. Every concept you have ever learned is based on the law of duality, which is the belief in two, or separation. But what if everything you have ever learned about the world is false, or based on a false concept? If the foundation of something is flawed then everything built upon that foundation is flawed as well. It will inevitably collapse and fall.

So once again, there is very little hope in you grasping the concept of non-duality intellectually, mainly because non-duality is not a concept. It is the experience of *what is and what has always been True*, and if you let this Truth penetrate your heart, like incense seeping through a cracked door, you will transcend every concept you have ever learned before now. Then you can put this book down and revel in what has always been true — the un-compromised experience of your innate wholeness.

It is the EXPERIENCE of non-duality we are focused on here, not the intellectual understanding of it.

But there is a danger I want to make you aware of right now, a trap you will fall into if you are not careful and alert. This thing we sometimes call ego, which is just the part of your mind that refuses to see the whole picture, is an expert at using spiritual concepts to deflect the experience this book seeks to inspire. You may hear a voice that whispers (or even screams): "why are you wasting your time with this nonsense," or even, "this is a waste of your time... close this book and move on." If you hear anything similar to this, rejoice! It means you are making progress. It also means that ego is worried about its survival, and well it should be. If you stay true to this course and integrate all these lessons, ego's grip will be reduced to nothing, and that is the thing it is most afraid of.

Let Me explain what happens when you try to grasp this subject intellectually but not experientially. You will begin building concepts around the subject of non-duality, convincing yourself that you know something that you did not know before, or that you understand concepts that eluded you until now. Then you will begin charting the course of differentiation — deciding who is teaching dualistic concepts and who is actually nondual. You will convince yourself that you can judge the difference, and you may even decide to confront those who you believe are teaching from a dualistic perspective.

Let Me take this opportunity to burst your bubble. *A nondual mind sees only the nondual, while the dualistic mind perceives only dualism. A Whole-Mind sees only wholeness while a split mind sees only illusions.* In other words, the idea that you can judge who is and who is not teaching non-dualism is the very thing that will keep you locked in the concepts of separation, all the while convincing you that you have made progress and are now the arbitrator of Oneness. Don't fall into that trap.

Please understand this point because it will save you years of self-deception — when you enter into the experience of nondual reality, that is all you will see — nondual reality — NO MATTER WHAT. Of course, you will be able to discern the difference between one who teaches from the unified field and one who teaches dualism, but it will not make the slightest bit of difference to you. It will not matter what another person says or the lessons they teach. You will experience only the nondual. That is all you will experience because *it is the only thing that experiences you* — and that is all that matters. The only thing that experiences you is YOU. That is the essence of non-dualism.

Here is a quick exercise that will help you understand this better. Lift your index finger about six or seven inches in front of your face and look directly at it. How many fingers do you see? One. Why? Because you are only holding up one finger. Now, instead of looking directly at your finger, pick a spot on the other side of the room and look at it. Make sure you are looking through your finger, not to the left or the right. How many fingers do you see now? Two? But are there *really* two fingers? No. You know that you are only holding up one finger, yet you perceive two. Now return your focus to your finger and notice that the two you perceived a moment ago have become one again.

The experience of non-dualism is nothing more than a shift in focus from two to one, or from what appears to be in front of you to what actually is. Let's look at this in another way.

Everything you have ever been taught since you were born into this world has been divided into two parts — that which is happening within you, or your inner life, and that which seems to be happening outside you, or your outer life. You are forced into making a distinction between your mind and matter, the within and the without. This is the essence of dualism, the idea that these two are separate and will never be joined.

The nondual experience is the opposite. It is not an idea or a concept but a tangible reality that cannot be challenged. Why can't it be challenged? This is a difficult question to answer since its unchallengeable nature lies in having a direct experience of a reality the mind will never be able to comprehend. Until you have had this direct experience you will believe what your senses tell you to believe. But once those beliefs have been challenged and you see through them or you see what is happening, you won't need to be convinced of anything. You will KNOW that there is no such thing as split-reality. You won't need evidence to support what you know to be true — that there is one reality that is whole and interconnected. The so-called evidence that seems to oppose this is simply disregarded in favor of the real.

Here is a fun example to illustrate what I mean. I own a set of VR glasses that has many games and programs that mimic reality in dramatic ways. One of them is called The Plank. I love to put the glasses on people to see how they react to this virtual world. It begins with them seeing themselves standing on a street with birds and butterflies and even helicopters flying overhead. It looks completely real. They then turn around and see an elevator with its door open, and when they walk inside (this is done physically) they see several buttons on the wall. I usually stand over the shoulder of the person experiencing the environment and tell them to push the button that says "Plank." They reach out their hand and push the button. As soon as they do the door closes and they see and feel themselves traveling the many floors to the top of the building.

This is where it gets interesting. Nearly everyone has the same reaction when the door opens again. They usually step back and gasp in horror or scream: "no way, I am not going." What they see is a plank that extends off the hundredth floor of the building straight out into the open air. It looks and feels completely real, and the reaction everyone has, even if they consciously know that it isn't real, is pure terror. Then they hear my voice over their shoulder say: "There is no reason to be afraid. It is not real and there is no way you can get hurt. Just step out onto the plank and walk as far as you can."

Watching people tip-toe onto an imaginary plank they perceive to be hundreds of feet above the ground is hilarious. Once again, they know intellectually that there is nothing to fear, that they never left the ground, but everything inside them says that they might fall to their death. Most people (but not all) get their courage up and take a few steps onto the plank, sometimes struggling to maintain their balance, then turn around and walk back into the elevator, push the button that says "ground." They then express deep gratitude when the door opens again and they are back on solid ground. It is only when they take off the glasses that their tension relaxes and they have a tangible experience of: I was never in any REAL danger.

This is very similar to what you will experience when you break free from the prison of dualism and enter the eternal space of non-duality. Wearing the VR glasses is virtual/virtual reality, twice removed from the Truth. Virtual reality is what you are experiencing right now, the experience of being separate from your Source, sometimes known as God, and everything else you perceive. The experience of your unified or nondual nature is like taking off the invisible glasses that are showing you a world that isn't real, the world where you compete with everything and everyone, where you are vulnerable to attack, and where you might lose your life at any moment.

It is impossible to lose your life in a virtual world, just like you were never in any danger of falling off the plank. And that is the experience this book is about to lead you toward — the eternal Presence we sometimes call I AM Consciousness that is whole and wholly protected. This will not happen through words or symbols, but through cracking open the egg you have been hiding inside for so long. You are like the baby bird that persistently pecks its tiny beak on the inside of the shell until it finally cracks and breaks open. Until then you project your beliefs about the world onto the inside of the shell, but the moment you are free to look around and see the Real World, you will never be able to claim those projections again.

The Challenge Of Words

Words may seem to describe what you experience as reality, but as you are about to discover, they are the very thing blocking you from seeing what is real. *A Course In Miracles* says that words are symbols of symbols, therefore they are twice removed from the Truth. A symbol of reality is never equal to reality itself. It may represent what it symbolizes but it will never be the same. That is why to truly understand non-duality you need to transcend the need for words, or at least lessen their priority.

At the same time, it would be a mistake to say that certain words describe the experience we seek while others block it. For example, I have met people who say that using the word *God* immediately blocks one from the experience of God. The word God, they would say, blocks the nondual experience. That is true, but only because they believe it is true. There are no words that will allow nor block the experiences of Oneness unless you want them to. The key is to use words for what they are useful for, but not give them undue value. It would be impossible to write a book about non-duality without using words, for example. But the words I am choosing are meant to untie the knots you have wrapped around yourself rather than reinforce them. This is an example of using words for what they are good for rather than for what they could never be good for.

Don't let anything block you from the experience this is meant to inspire. The choice is yours. The purpose of this book is to use words for what they are useful for, then to let them dissolve in the experience of your True Nature.

How To Read This Book

The rest of this book is divided into short sections that will help you penetrate the dualistic world you have believed in until now. Each section is an expression of the nondual experience, and even though words are utilized to stimulate this experience, they should not be given more value than the feelings they activate. As you slowly read each section you will feel something beginning to move inside you, similar to an unborn child stirring in its mother's womb. As you continue to open yourself to this stirring you may feel stronger shifts taking place. It may even be confusing or difficult at first, but don't stop moving forward. Trusting the Light contained in each section is enough to help you break free from your self-imposed prison cell.

Commit to reading at least one section per day. This determination will serve you well. And as you read each one, give yourself the space to let it settle within you, growing roots that sink deep into your consciousness. And remember that the Truth within you knows the path that leads to the home you never really left. You would do well to trust that path now because it is about to lead you back to You, the Reality that has always been Real.

Finally, resist the urge to judge what you are about to read with your intellectual mind. Drink each lesson in like it is fine wine. Don't rush and don't push. If you read something that causes fear or even anger, hold still and try to go deeper. Remember, your ego is going to want to push these lessons away and convince you not to trust them. I can promise you from my own experience, as well as the experience of hundreds of people who have already taken this course, that this gives you everything you need to break free from ego's dream of separation into the eternal vastness of Heaven.

So, what are you waiting for? Take your first step out onto the plank and feel the open air. I promise, there is no danger here.

Clarification Of Terms

Throughout this book, you will come across references to "I AM." This refers to the name of God that was given to Moses at the burning bush, a shortened version of "I AM That, I AM." When you read the words I AM in these lessons it refers to the Presence of the Divine within you or the Presence of God. Once again, it is important to be gentle with words and concepts since none of them can completely contain the essence of the experience we are here to receive. Many people are triggered by words like *God* and *Spirit* since they believe they refer to something outside of themselves. This is only true if you believe it is. You could just as easily use the word *God* or the words *I AM* to refer to the limitless, all-encompassing nondual Reality that is forever Real and Whole. Once again, your experience of such words is what you choose to experience and nothing else.

The only important thing to remember is that the I AM Presence within you is One with God now and forever. By God, we are referring to the eternal, changeless source of ALL Reality, not a deity or a being outside of YOU. Keep this in mind as you move through these lessons.

A Whole Answer

The Real cannot die; the unreal has never lived. What I AM has always existed and remains forever as it is and always will be.

What is this I AM? It is the very essence you have denied but which has never denied you. It is the immovable center of all creation where you find your Being.

Are there many expressions of this I AM?

Though appearing in many forms, the I AM is One, and though expressing itself through an infinite number of lenses, it emerges from a single source of Light. As a beam of light passes through a prism and separates into a multitude of colors, so does the I AM express itself through an uncountable number of souls while always remaining One within Itself.

Where is this I AM Presence? Everywhere expressed and eternally known, the ocean of I AM contains all, excludes none, and remains whole though expressed through many tongues. And yet no tongue can speak it, no instrument can play it and no container can contain it. Why? Because it remains forever beyond all description. It is everywhere you look and everywhere you are seen.

You are everywhere you look as well — the Truth of who you are and forever will remain. Choose to See what has always Seen you and you will realize the Truth that has always been True. There is nothing left for you to do but realize this. You have been called into an intimate embrace that eclipses the world you believed was real, and your answer to this call will determine whether you are ready to accept or reject this embrace. But you cannot reject it forever since it would never reject you. And since you are that which has never rejected your Self, the task was complete before it was ever conceived.

Exercise

"Choose to See what has always Seen you."

This one line expresses what we are calling The Nondual Universe. And yet, when you fully embrace these words and the lessons contained within this course it will no longer be a theory, but a full and natural experience. It is natural because it is inherently True, though until now you have accepted an illusion of reality that denies this Truth. You have been told that you are vulnerable and easily attacked. These lessons teach that you are invulnerable and that it is impossible to wound what has no opposite. If you choose to realize or See this, then you will discover that it has always Seen you. You are and have always been recognized by the single Source of ALL Reality, and this cannot be challenged or denied. You may seem to deny it for a moment, but that which is True remains as it has always been, so resistance is ultimately futile.

Spend at least ten minutes today choosing to See this reality. This is a gift that was freely given to you, and now you must learn to freely give what you have received. Look around yourself now. If you are in a restaurant choose to See everyone as they sit eating their meals or talking to each other. See them as they are Seen in Reality, what we sometimes call God. Remember, any gift you give to another is given to yourself, so feel this gift return to you. Choose to See yourself now, the True Self that is always Seen by God. The more you give this to others the more you will realize that nothing else exists. And when you fully embrace the only thing that truly exists you will realize that it has always embraced you.

Learn How To Dissolve

If you want the Truth to increase within you, learn how to dissolve. Focus on stepping back into the mystery if you want to move forward into the Kingdom.

The ways of the world are not the ways of God. The way of the seen is not a path to the unseen. Everything you were told about saving your life is the opposite of the Truth. Give your life away and you will discover your True Life. Surrender what the world claims and you will be claimed by God.

Whatever you cling to will increase. If you cling to illusions they will manifest everywhere. But illusions are what they are because they are hard to distinguish from the Truth. If you cling only to love, your life will be used to manifest miracles, then it will be easy to see through that which was never real.

Exercise

The I AM Presence is where you are NOW. The moment has arrived when this experience can be known and never forgotten. It begins by claiming the I AM Presence, and this is done simply by calling upon the name and essence of God using the words: I AM. Sit for no less than ten minutes and rest in this Presence. Repeat this phrase until you feel it take root in your soul:

"I AM where love is NOW."

Feel the confidence of this growing within you and let it come into your mind throughout the day.

The Will Of God Is Beyond Change

The life you think you lead has been stitched together by fear, but the life you truly lead, that which is known by God, is fashioned and maintained by love. The life you have been focusing on until now will end, and it is the idea of this ending that makes you fearful. But the idea of an ending is nothing more than that — an idea. Shift your focus from that which seems to end — the personality and the body — to that which has no beginning and no end, and fear disappears on its own.

That which seems to end is not known by God since the heart of God is eternal and you are held within God's heart. God knows only the real and reality remains as it has always been. Likewise, you remain as you have always been and that is why sickness, pain, and death are illusions in your mind attempting to prove that you can change the will of God. The will of God is beyond change, just as the truth of your eternal identity IN God is beyond change. Trust this and fear will vanish forever.

It is time to release all the ideas that have captured your mind and convinced you of your littleness. The Light in you is brighter than a thousand suns, but you have reduced it in your mind to the point that it is hardly seen at all. However, this reduction you claim is an impossible dream that does not affect reality. Accept this fully, for it has already fully accepted you.

Exercise

Until now you have accepted ego's version of you which is nothing more than a shadow meant to deny the Truth within. But you can turn away from that shadow, back toward the Light, whenever you choose. So choose NOW. There is nothing left to wait for. Nothing is going to come along that will offer you more than *everything*. There is no such thing as more than everything no matter what you have been led to believe until now. Spend several moments in quiet contemplation of these words throughout the day:

"I AM Everything in One".

These words alone have the power to undo all the illusions you have chosen to believe, replaced by the only reality you have ever truly KNOWN.

A True Spiritual Path

The joy you are feeling is the result of you losing your need to hold your thoughts together in a sequential time association. That would have felt like death a moment ago, and it would have been, just not the death of anything real. It would have been the death of the unreality you have claimed until now, the 'unreal you,' and until now that has been very frightening. You were afraid of losing yourself, but the fear you were experiencing was the only thing blocking you from realizing that the *you* you were afraid of losing was never real. It was nothing more than the accumulation of separating attack thoughts.

You can only see how insane this thought is when you look directly at it! Why would you want to be an accumulation of separating attack thoughts? You can only want that if you are not conscious of what you really want. Do you see that? You can only want the unreal if you don't realize it is an illusion. You can only choose a dream over reality if you forget that it is a dream. The instant you realize that you have been seeking a non-existent reality you will give it up, but only when you have a direct experience of what Reality actually is. In other words, you can not want what IS until you release your tight grip on what is not.

That is the only thing a Whole-Mind is here to get you to do, LET GO of what is not. What is not has never been. That should make sense even to your intellectual mind. Likewise, what IS has always been. This is harder to comprehend since the concept of 'never been' is easier to comprehend than the reality of 'always been.' Ego-mind is bound by time so it refuses to accept the eternal, forcing the same rules upon your mind. But it can do so only as long as you allow it to. The instant you choose to see through the eyes of your Whole-Mind the world you thought you see disappears and is replaced by the Real World where One is One and nothing else exists.

Exercise

Ego or split-mind believes that two is two, or that it is possible to split the reality of One. The transformation of your mind from a perceptual lens to seeing through the eyes of God is as simple as realizing that Oneness is shared by all, and yet it remains forever whole. This is something the intellectual mind can never understand, and yet you can feel this truth when you relax into the experience of One. Spend time saying these words as often as you can today:

"I AM One, I AM One."

You may begin to feel the experience of this Oneness taking hold of you. Let it. Don't block the Light that is beginning to shine through the dark shadows of your mind. Keep saying these words until you KNOW that they are true.

An Unpopular Spiritual Path

People have been led to believe that the most popular spiritual path is the right one to follow. What I am telling you is very different. If a spiritual path is popular it is probably the wrong path for you to take.

A True Path is and will always be unpopular because it requires so much of you. It requires that you give ALL of yourself, while the popular path asks you to only give some or most of yourself. I am not talking about giving all your money to a charismatic leader or a church. I am telling you that if you want to be free you must be willing to give everything to Everything, and there is no popular spiritual path on the planet that goes that far. Why? Because popular spiritual paths are designed to keep you bound to this world, not release you from it. They are popular because they offer the illusion of spiritual growth but never the real thing. They teach the use of spiritual law to help you accumulate goods rather than goodness, or riches instead of richness. This distracts you from the only path that has True Power — the unpopular path that requires you to give everything to Everything.

Exercise

This is where the distinction between ego's version of a spiritual path and a true spiritual path becomes clear. Are you seeking to gain more of something or ALL of EVERYTHING? The first path is easy for the intellectual mind to comprehend, but the second is impossible. And that is how we recognize it for what it is — wholly beyond the rational mind.

The rational mind sees only a small part of the picture but your Whole-Mind sees the entire picture at once. You are capable of this NOW if you allow yourself to be. Until now you have limited your vision of reality because you thought that you were limited. You are unlimited now and forever, and it is time for you to accept this. So spend time today releasing ego's hold on what it believes to be true and see if you can receive the WHOLE answer you have been seeking. You do not know how to do this, and you do not have to. But there is ONE who does know, you are being asked to surrender into this ONE now. See if you can get a feel for this today and let the richness of your soul overflow into the world you perceive.

What You Already Know

If only you realized what you already Know, every question in your mind would instantly dissolve. You wouldn't even care if your questions were answered because you would realize that they are all meaningless. Only the answer remains, an answer without a question. Until now YOU were the question because you were confused about your own reality or who you are in the sight of God. But now that you know who you are — the perfect extension of Love Itself — you know your Self to be the only answer you need. When you Truly Know this, freedom from limited self-identity is complete.

Realizing what you already Know is as simple as opening your eyes and choosing to See what has always been right in front of you. Until now you have chosen to "not" see this because you were afraid of what it might mean. Let Me end the mystery once and for all: it means that you are the very essence of love no matter what the so-called evidence seems to portray. Trust Me when I tell you that opening your eyes and seeing your True Self shining in all its glory is not painful. Every symbol of pain disappears in this light, replaced by a world where everything you deserve has always been yours.

Exercise

Realizing what you already know begins by admitting that you do not know anything. Does that sound strange? *Surely there are a few things I know to be true*, you will say to yourself. You interpret *not knowing* as weakness or failure when the opposite is true. Admitting that you were mistaken about reality opens the door to glimpse what cannot be seen by human eyes or touched by human hands. The soul alone is capable of this type of knowledge, and it begins by releasing everything you have relied on until now.

Close your eyes and take several deep breaths, and as you do, see if you can release your concepts of the world you think you see and simply rest in the Real World that surrounds you this and every moment. At first, this may feel difficult or strange but as you continue to rest here you will feel an openness that transcends the world. When you arrive in this sacred place speak these words:

"I AM Known by God."

Repeat these words over and over until you feel a rush of insight. Everything you need is contained within this I AM current and it will not fail you if you choose to release all the illusions you have carried until now.

The Mind And Healing

Healing the body of illness or disease is natural when you realize that illness and disease occur first in the mind, then manifest in the body. Therefore, what requires healing is the idea that you require healing. This begins as a thought which is then accepted by the mind, but that is only the first step. The thought then takes root, sinking deep into the ground of consciousness until it grows strong enough to overcome the weeds of the split-mind that suffocates the Truth.

What you give value to will seem valuable. This is such a simple thought but the effect it has on your life is immeasurable. It seems strange because you do not give enough value to the mind which manifests both disease and healing. It is, in fact, where true value resides.

The intellect neither creates nor heals, but only accepts what has already been accepted by God. But the mind does have the power to reject what has been accepted by God. This is what you call freedom of choice, but only one of these choices has a true effect. In other words, the decision to either accept or reject what has been accepted by God is yours, but you cannot make them both Real. What is Real is forever True, and what is not real is an illusion and cannot become real simply because you want it to.

Choose apart from what has been accepted by God and you have made a choice that has no real effect. This is because you cannot create beyond that which was created by God. It is impossible, though you seem determined to do it anyway. Likewise, you cannot create yourself but you CAN either accept or reject your Reality. If you accept it fully you will see that it has already fully accepted you, and perfect healing will result. If you deny the Truth of who you are you will reject the perfect love which accepts you perfectly. As always, it is your choice. Trust who you are — that which is seen and loved by God — and the choice will be easy.

Exercise

You have a choice: what has been chosen by God or reject what God chooses. As you have learned, it is not a real choice but only a decision about what you want to experience. If you choose with God you will receive blessings upon blessings that transcend everything you have ever learned about the world. If you choose against these blessings you will only be denying yourself what has always been yours. Once again, this is the illusion of a choice, but it will feel very real.

See if you can identify some of the ways you have chosen against God's choice. Remember, what God chooses always brings peace and harmony, so it should be easy to notice the difference. What decisions have you made that brought discord or lack of peace? As soon as you identify one or two of these, choose again. Relax into the decision for grace, the desire for holiness, and the longing for the experience of Oneness. This is how you will enter into the Nondual Universe, and it is how you will remain there for all eternity.

You Are Already Healed

If you want to be healed, release all your thoughts and ideas of what it means to be healed. None of them can help you, but releasing them opens the door to the experience of being *already healed*.

Healing on any level occurs on its own when you realize that there is only one level — the level of Spirit. It does not matter if you seem to require healing on a physical, mental or emotional level. They are all the same to Spirit, and when they are all the same to you, you will know what it means to be whole, and everything whole is wholly healed.

Exercise

Everything whole is wholly healed. This is Gospel or very good news. It speaks directly to this lesson, the fact that healing has already occurred and your only role is to allow it to be true. The fact that it is already true should help you. All of these exercises lead here — to the tangible experience of what is now, what always has been, and what always will be true. What do you feel when you read those words? Does it fill you with a sense of hope the world will never comprehend? Or does it make you feel afraid as if something will be lost if you accept everything? Spend a few moments examining your reaction to the phrase:

"Everything whole is wholly healed."

Accept These Truths Without Reservation

If you want to learn what it means to live in the nondual universe, accept these three truths without reservation:

1. That God IS, but what God is is completely beyond your rational mind. If you give up the need to understand that which can never be understood by the intellectual mind you will be able to receive the gift of Knowledge. You will simply Know what God is, though you will never be able to explain it with words. This is the pearl beyond any price, and it is only this you should seek now.

2. That the nature of God is love, but not the love you have claimed until now. Once again, your intellectual mind can only reach so far, and the eternal nature of love is forever beyond your reach. But it is not beyond the reach of your *experience* if you choose to see everything as God Sees. God Sees everything as inseparable from love, and once again, you would do well to seek this same vision.

3. The nature of God is to extend that which it knows Itself to Be. You have convinced yourself that you can create or extend beyond your nature. You can not. If God's nature is love and you are

forever united in that love, then love is all you can extend or nothing at all. That is the only choice you have — extend what and who you are or extend nothing at all. Only one of these is creative. Extending nothing, which is what you have tried to do until now, is only the illusion of creativity.

This is the Truth about God, but you will not experience this Truth unless you realize it is also the Truth about you. Until then you will try in vain to separate from the inseparable. Until then you will believe that love is something you need to gain rather than realize that love is the very foundation of your existence.

Exercise

Trying to separate from the inseparable causes confusion and fear. Is it any wonder that the world manifests these feelings and worse? The desire to solve problems in the world is tempting but it will only cause more confusion. Begin by solving the problem in your mind. The solution is simple — there never was a REAL problem to solve. When you become the living embodiment of this you will do more to heal the world and everyone in it than you ever could before. You are called to be an instrument of peace, but an instrument doesn't play itself. It allows itself to be played, and this is what you are calling forth now.

Spend time in prayer today asking to be shown how you can be used as an instrument of peace. It begins by being willing to accept this yourself, then the next step will be to share what you have received. Be like the vibrating strings of a harp tuned to Divine frequencies. If this becomes your only goal then the music issuing from your soul will lead many others into the nondual universe you are beginning to enjoy.

Look Softly Upon The World

Let your hold on this world be tenuous. Look with soft eyes upon all created things and you will begin to perceive the creative force behind everything. It is like looking into a mirror and forgetting that the one you see in front of you is the one who is seeing, or realizing that the reflection is nothing, while the ONE being reflected is everything. Just relax and look upon this ONE and feel the love that always looks upon you.

Exercise

Today's exercise is simple — see how it feels to hold everything you perceive in this world lightly, without attachment or expectation. You will find that it is impossible to do this all at once because you have gained such proficiency at claiming the world of form thinks it will give you something you don't already have. Try to loosen your grip today and get a sense of how it feels to live so openly.

The reason you hold the world so tight is that you are afraid you won't survive if you don't. Giving everything to receive everything creates a feeling of loss inside you. The reason is simple: you were told that accepting everything requires a sacrifice, but when you look at this idea clearly, you discover that it is insane. You have been listening to this insane voice for far too long and now it is time to let go and trust the Voice that knows what you really want and deserve.

So once again, see how it feels to loosen your grip on the attachments you hold so dear and come with wholly empty hands unto God.

A Riddle Leading To The Truth

Realize who you are and you will automatically stop trying to convince yourself that *who you are* is vulnerable to attack. It is *who you are not* that is vulnerable to attack, and since *who you are not* does not really exist, the Truth of you is wholly protected this and every moment. Realizing that you are wholly protected this and every moment is what the Holy Instant is, and when you live fully within the Holy Instant you will realize that it always lives fully within you.

These may sound like riddles to your mind right now, but the day is coming when their meaning will be completely clear. It is unclear now because you are still unclear about your identity and your true function. My job is to keep tapping this message into your mind until it becomes completely clear.

Imagine someone tapping Morse Code onto your hand before you are capable of understanding how to unlock the code's meaning. It is impossible to understand at first but if the tapping goes on for days, weeks, or even years, the meaning will become clear. That is exactly what I AM doing — I AM tapping a Divine Code into your mind that is impossible for you to fully comprehend right now, but the moment is coming when it will be simple to unlock, and when this happens you will look back and realize that the message was so simple: you are loved now and forever.

And here is how you can work around the seeming effort it takes to unlock the code — simply accept that you are loved now and forever without reservation. That is all you need to do and the code will no longer be needed. You will realize and remember the truth that has always been true, that YOU have always been YOU.

Exercise

You are loved now and forever! Isn't this what you want? To know that this love is unconditional, not based on any need or demand, is what you have been longing for without realizing it. Now the question is, how do you fully receive this gift and experience its Reality?

The answer is very simple — become the source of the same gift to everyone you meet. You don't need to say a word unless you choose to. All you need to do is be willing to See as God Sees and to Know what God Knows. God sees only the love that rests at the core of your being, and God knows that you are lovable no matter what the outer conditions of the world seem to be. Are you willing to see others in the same way? If you are then this gift will grow inside you until it overflows into the world, and even beyond this world you see.

Once again, all that is required is your willingness to be the source of the love that is being offered to you now. It takes practice looking past all the errors ego forces upon you, but as you become more and more adept at this, the shift will become easy because the joy you feel will overwhelm the fear.

An Unreasonable Truth

Expecting the Truth to be intellectually reasonable is completely unreasonable. Truth does not, as a rule, appeal to your sense of reason since Truth exists beyond all worldly reason. If it seems to do so then you have to ask yourself this question: is this really the Truth or simply what I want to be true? In most cases, if it appeals to your mind, you will discover it was the latter.

Always be suspicious of a truth that seems reasonable. It is like a mask that draws attention to unreal features rather than the soft, subtle features that lie beneath the mask. The Truth is always what lies beneath or behind the illusion of the mask.

There is no idea or concept of the Truth that can approach the Truth Itself. But there is a feeling that is associated with or inspired by the Truth that gives you the sense of Reality. This Reality is always the Reality of love, nothing more and nothing less. It is a love that is forever present and forever felt, but when you seek an intellectual understanding of this Truth it evades you, while the feeling pulls you forward, like the scent of a rare flower that draws you deeper into the garden.

Exercise

The mind or ego searches constantly for the concept of truth and does whatever it can to make it seem reasonable — or in alignment with what it already believes to be true. What ego finds completely unreliable is a Truth that is always True. It prefers a version of the truth that changes when expressed through different people or in different situations. Have you ever heard someone say: *"We all have our own truths"*? That statement seems very reasonable to the part of your mind that doesn't understand who you *really* are, but it is completely unreasonable to the Truth Itself.

In other words, there is only ONE Truth, but you will never be able to comprehend it in a world of changing forms. It can only be experienced in the nondual universe we are entering now.

Make a list of the supposed truths that seem reasonable to your mind. Perhaps you will decide that it is reasonable for people to have different ideas about the ultimate truth, or that alternative truths are possible. Examine these ideas from the lens of *The Single Truth* that is incomprehensible to ego. For example, ego believes that what is true for one may not be true for another. This is what we would call a relative truth, one that changes from person to person. But this is not the level of Truth we are seeking now. Do you believe that Truth can be the same for everyone, and yet the experience of this Truth is impossible to achieve in a world of relativity? If so, you are getting closer to stepping outside ego's concept of truth into the Truth that is known by God.

The 3 Most Important Words You Will Ever Say (And Mean)

The healing of your mind from the illusory world happens automatically when you say and truly mean these three words: "I AM Here" since *here* is the only place it is possible for you to be. Do you see how simple this is? The thought "I once was there" (past) or "I will soon be there" (future) is the source of all your discomfort, and it is the only thing that blocks you from entering the nondual universe.

When we say you are *here* it does not refer to where your body stands, sits, or seems to exist. It has nothing to do with your body but everything to do with your True Identity. Yes, even your body can only be in one place and that is why this realization brings about a whole healing. We use the words "whole healing" to differentiate it from the partial healing you have preferred until now. You say "I want to be healed of this cancer," or "I am praying to be healed of this disease," but what you refuse to realize is that there is no such thing as being healed partially. Even if the cancer disappears, or you are healed of a particular disease, it comes back at a later date or is replaced by another ailment that allows you to keep the contract you made with ego before time began — that you can choose to die. Is it beginning to seem strange that you made such a bargain? What benefit did you receive from seeming to prove that you are an identity contained within a body that ultimately must grow old, decay, and die?

"This is just the way of things," you believe. "Everything must ultimately pass away." That is true if you decide that you are a body and that you are held within the right grip of the body's limitations. I AM here to simply tell you that none of that is true. You are not subject to any of these limitations unless you choose to be. You could just as easily choose to see yourself as God sees you, which is limitless, beyond all sickness and disease, and untouched by death.

Why not start now? Why not be here, the only place you actually are?

Exercise

Yes, why not start now? You may be asking yourself how to do that. This lesson spells it out perfectly. Just say these words and give them your whole attention:

"I AM Here."

This means more than you likely realize. It means that the I AM Presence is here as you in this very moment. It has nothing to do with whether you realize that fact in your mind, only that it is absolutely True regardless of your belief or knowledge of the Truth. The I AM is Present through and as you NOW. Claim this by saying the words:

"I AM Here."

Let the reality behind these words remove all the blocks that have kept you hidden in the shadows until now.

Let Go And Let God

Release the mental struggle and the need to know and simply allow yourself to be Known. Let go of the intellectual desire to understand and simply allow yourself to be Understood. The Truth within you is always Known and Understood by God but you have made the decision (though you forgot that it was YOUR decision) to not know or understand your True Self, or your REALITY, choosing instead to think it is possible to know that which could never be Known by God. But here is the problem: what can never be Known by God can never be Known by you, though you refuse to fully accept this. You have created an illusory sense of knowledge, or knowing yourself, but the *self* you think you *know* is not real. It is like believing you know or understand a shadow. Shadows can never be known or understood. But that which casts the shadow is always Known.

Once again, let go of the struggle and the struggle lets go of you. Stop trying to wrap your mind around something that could never be real and let Reality wrap itself around you. The difference between these two experiences will be felt immediately. It is like walking out of a dark room into the sunlight. There is no denying the shift, just as there is no denying the difference between a dark room and standing outside on a sunny day — unless you refuse to See. If your eyes are closed you will be confused by the shift. If your eyes are closed you may not witness the full evidence of your decision to leave a room filled with shadows.

You are being called to open your eyes and SEE that which has always been SEEN by God. Anything that God Sees can and will be Seen by you, it is just a matter of time. Actually, it is just a matter of being released *from* time.

Why not now?

Exercise

Are you willing to finally let go of the struggle to make a shadow real? This is what you do whenever you claim to be vulnerable and weak, or that your reality is based on your physical existence. But now you have been given the chance to open your eyes and See who you are in Truth — that the Truth in you is loved by an eternally loving Creator. You can choose to relate to this Creator however you want. It may help to know that none of the images you will use are real, but that does not matter. The only thing that matters is your willingness to turn away from the shadow you claimed as your reality and See yourself — your True Self — as God Sees you. God Sees you for who you are, not the shadow you imagine yourself to be.

Spend some time asking to be released from the fearful images you have claimed about your identity. You can not do this on your own; asking for help is the only way you will accomplish this task. It is the only thing you need to do at this point — ask for guidance then follow the guidance you receive. If you are at the point where you are ready to release your tight grip on the shadow world where you seem to be separate from ALL THAT IS, ask to be shown the path into this experience. There are powerful allies all around you. All you need to do is ask for help, and help will be given to you.

Enlightenment And Healing

Spiritual Enlightenment, or stepping into the nondual universe, means perceiving spiritual reality where human concepts seem to be. Spiritual healing means perceiving what is whole where illness seems to be. Do you see how these are the same? Enlightenment requires seeing through the *seeming* reality to reality itself. Healing requires looking past what *seems* to require healing to what could never be in reality. This is the Vision of God! This is how God sees! And it is also how God heals. And you can do the same — but only if it is your ONE desire.

Exercise

Claim the Vision of God today. Is it so simple? It is if you want it to be. All *you* need to do is be willing to step away from that which has always stepped away from you. Illusions are like shadows. Have you ever walked away from a shadow that was cast upon the wall? What happened? The shadow walked away from you as you walked away from it. But the Truth always walks toward you, not away, because the Truth is all there is. So once again, claim the Vision of God today. You do not need instructions on how to do this. All you need is the willingness to lay down the sword you used to fight a winless battle. I promise that the instant you lay down this sword the Light will come streaming in from every direction.

Step Into Heaven

Stop trying to hear this message with your ears. It is impossible for you to grasp these words. Stop trying to understand this message with your mind. The mind can never ascend to such heights.

"I have come to take you home."

That is all you need to know. It does not matter that it is a home you never really left. All that is important is that I AM here NOW and My hand is reaching out to you this and every moment.

It is up to you to receive this gift. It is up to you to decide if you want to step out of the world that never gave you what you wanted. Why would you choose to remain in a world that has never truly welcomed you? You are being welcomed into Heaven at this very moment, but you must choose to enter. It is an experience you can enjoy now, not after you choose to lay your body aside. You can stand at the gate lifetime after lifetime, but the step I AM calling you to take is so small. Reach out and take my hand and I will guide you perfectly into the home you never left except in your imagination.

Exercise

If you hang around Me long enough you will hear Me say these words:

"You never actually left Heaven except in

your imagination."

I am not referring to the idea of Heaven most of us were raised with. There is no such place as a kingdom with pearly gates and streets lined with gold. But there is a reality you can enjoy, a state of unified consciousness that is always available to you. You can call that reality Heaven if you want, or anything else. Words will never come close to describing this state of Oneness, but you can enjoy it now simply because it is a state that has never truly been challenged.

Choose Heaven and the experience of Heaven will dawn upon your mind. This experience is not something you have to die to gain, as you have been told. It is a state of consciousness you achieve when you give up the need to die. Read that last sentence again: *a state of consciousness you achieve when you give up the need to die.* Is such an experience available to you? Tune in and see how you feel when you say the words aloud. Say:

"I choose to enjoy the consciousness of

Heaven now."

How does it feel within? Do you feel an expansion or a contraction?

My guess is that something takes root and grows within every time you say these words and really mean them. And if this feels like something you want to continue to enjoy, just stay with these lessons. They are meant to undo all the strange beliefs that linger in your mind, all the ideas and concepts that have kept you locked in hell.

The First Position

There is no difference between Me and anyone who lives, except that I know who I AM. This Knowledge allows Me to move through time and space without changing. It is the changeless that moves without moving, the unborn giving birth to Itself. This is who I AM and will forever remain. I claim it now, just as it has always claimed Me.

You speak to Me but that which I AM neither hears nor answers. It simply rests within the Answer. You call to Me but I neither respond nor move from where I AM now, for where I AM now is the only place I can be. And I See you resting in the same Illumined Reality since the *you* you seem to be is nothing, while the You that is Known cannot exist outside of Me. We are One within the Heart and Mind of Eternal Love, and that is the only thing there is for Me to Know.

In the world of events, questions rise and answers seem to follow. But where I AM there are no questions, only perfect certainty of Self. This certainty is not something that can be earned through effort or will. It is a gift that is offered this and every moment. All I need is the willingness to empty my arms of the heavy load I have been carrying and accept what I AM offering. Every concept must be challenged and released before I can perceive this gift. Every attachment must dissolve before I can receive what has always been mine.

Read this lesson again and Know that it is only You speaking to Yourself, for the I AM can be nowhere but where you are now.

Exercise

Who do you think is speaking in this lesson? Is it a person or an enlightened being? Or is it You — the You that is fully illumined now and forever? This Presence, the I AM Presence, is the Truth of who you are. It neither changes nor adapts to change. It is the eternal within you that is waking up within the radiance of Heaven.

Today's practice is simple: allow this radiance to shine in you and touch everyone you see or even think of. You can do this simply by being willing to lay aside anything that appears to contradict the reality you share with all beings everywhere. This willingness is the lesson and the practice today. It cracks open the door and allows in enough Light to penetrate the dream, stirring you from your sleep. And as you awaken, you will see the Light everywhere for it is everywhere and in everyone. The Light has come into your mind and now it is yours to see it everywhere.

The First Position, Pt. 2

There is only one position where I AM, the First Position. No position exists but this, and so it is impossible for Me to be anywhere but HERE.

And yet, you have created an alternative in your mind where there is none. The illusion of this alternative manifests within a dream state you mistake for reality. This illusion is the denial of the Oneness which is the only possible reality. It is the only possible reality because God is ONE and there is nothing outside of All That Is. Therefore, denying this denial is the first step to releasing the tight grip of the split mind. Denying ego's denial of Oneness allows a gap to manifest in your mind that interrupts the flow of illusory concepts. Without a consistent flow of illusions, the veil begins to dissolve and part on its own, then you will be able to see past ego's façade.

This is the point of no return. When you finally perceive what ego's façade hides, you will automatically lose faith in the illusions you mistook for reality. How can you believe in the power of a shadow after you realize it is nothing but a shadow? And when you lose faith in ego's illusory world, it dissolves on its own.

Exercise

This lesson begins by describing the First Position which is the only true position since the I AM Presence is everywhere and within everyone. The concept of multiple positions is the same as the belief in separation, a belief that is beginning to fade in your mind. This has nothing to do with the body you seem to inhabit or the personality you seem to possess. There seems to be an endless supply of separate bodies and objects, all of which seem to be outside your body. But the same is true in the dreams you experience when you are sleeping at night. It is only when you awaken from the dream that you realize it was all a fabrication within the mind so convincing that you took it for reality.

Look around yourself right now, wherever you are reading or listening to this book. Look at the people who are near you and see if you can sense a common thread of Light connecting you to each one of them. Let this golden thread vibrate like the strings of a guitar sending Light to everyone you see. You might believe that this is nothing more than an exercise, but I promise it is so much more. If you stay with this simple practice you will feel energy building within you, energy you may not be able to describe but which you somehow recognize. Do this throughout the day until it becomes a normal practice, allowing you to see through the illusion of separation to the interconnectedness of the soul.

The Remembrance Of God

Your belief in the restrictions of time is the only thing blocking you from the timeless remembrance of Heaven. You have been led to believe that growing old is inevitable. Why? Because every time the earth circles the sun you seem to age one year, and you are only allotted a certain number of years before your life ends. But what if you learned that your True Life has nothing to do with the spinning of planets or the passing of time? What if you realized that what holds remembrance of God is eternal? Would you celebrate this realization or would you continue to hide from that which has never been hidden from you?

So now the question becomes: What is it that has never been hidden from you? And here is the answer: The remembrance of God is what you are! Take a deep breath and proclaim this truth out loud:

"The remembrance of God is what I AM."

If this is true for you it must also be true for everyone you perceive. Why, then, would you look upon anyone with anything less than love? Regardless of the circumstance or what you believe, this is the reality that is forever real. And what is forever real is not bound by the limits of time.

This can only mean one thing: You are not bound by the limits of time or anything else in this world — UNLESS YOU CHOOSE TO BE! Indeed, this is what you have chosen — to believe you are limited, not limitless, which leads to the next inevitable belief — that you are guilty, not innocent. But now a revelation — you can choose again! This is all you are being called to do — make the choice that leads to your freedom, not your bondage. You can do it this very instant if you want. All that remains is for you to want it above everything in this world.

Exercise

As you just read, your desire is the key to experiencing the Truth that is forever True. Until now you have chosen to believe the illusions that could never be true, and because you believe them, they seem to affect on your life. If you believe that you are a body that can get sick, grow old and finally die, then you will experience that, even though the opposite is true. The Truth in you is not subject to any of the limitations of your body unless you choose to experience those limitations.

Now that you recognize this choice — choose again. Choose to see the timeless, limitless reality that is God's gift to you. And make sure you give this same gift to everyone you meet. Today's exercise is simple: make the choice of freedom, not bondage, and share the same. Choose to see what is right in front of you rather than the illusions that could never be real. You may need to make this choice many times before the experience breaks through your consciousness. But every time you make this decision the light will grow a little brighter in your mind and the world you thought was so solid and real will begin to appear less dense and dangerous. Welcome this vision, just as it has always welcomed you.

The Distant Horizon

Eternity is a reality held within the mind of God, therefore it is also in your mind. There is only one difference — the experience of your eternal nature is buried beneath all the illusions you have claimed until now, and so it seems to be limited or somehow contained. You are still unable to fully accept that God's eternal nature is your own, therefore death cannot be real. If eternal life is True for God then it must also be true for all.

Imagine standing on an ocean beach looking out toward the horizon. It seems that the water suddenly drops in the distance as if the earth is flat, and it wasn't very long ago that everyone in the world believed this to be true. Is this any different than believing God's grace is limited, or that the illusion of life's end, or death, is real? A few hundred years ago people believed that if they sailed their ships too far they would drop off the edge of the earth. Today people believe their lives will end when they reach the edge of their conceptual world. But is this true? All it took was one ship sailing further than what appeared to be the edge of the world to realize that the earth is round and that the edge or the ending was an illusion. And all it takes for you to realize that there is no death is the example of one who conquered death, demonstrating that the Truth within each one of us is eternal.

Just remember this: God's eternal nature is yours now and forever. Nothing can change this fact, especially a dream or an illusion.

Exercise

What limitations do you believe you are bound by? Perhaps you think you are not holy or good enough to awaken into wholeness, and you affirm this belief by harnessing the energy of God's name:

"I AM THAT"

to make it real. Today we are going to identify some of those limiting beliefs and turn the table on them. For example, using the example above, if you believe that you need to be holy to realize your wholeness, affirm this by saying:

"I AM Holy"

until you begin to feel the shift in your consciousness. You may even complete the phrase by saying:

"I AM Holy, I AM."

When you breathe in, imagine you are inhaling air from Heaven or the grace of eternity. Spend time with this today, as often as you remember, and see if you get a sense of your own Divinity.

The Unreal Shadow

Your determination to see what is not really there has convinced you that *nothing* can exist. *Nothing* can't exist and the instant you realize that you will open your eyes and SEE the Real World. You look at a shadow and claim it is alive. It moves and it dances, but never on its own. A shadow is nothing more than the manifestation of blocked light, which is exactly what your self-identity is. Does knowing the *you* you believe you are doesn't exist make you feel angry? Or does it fill you with profound joy? If you feel the approach of this joy then you are very close to breaking free from the chains that have held your identity in place for so long.

A shadow has no life of its own, but you can certainly imagine it does. Your imagination has the power to see whatever it wants to see, but it can't make the unreal real. That is beyond your power, and you are only now beginning to realize that. The more you realize this fact, the more obvious the Real World will become.

Until now you have been afraid to look at this but a sufficient amount of Light has come into your mind for you to See what has always been Seen by

God. What has always been Seen by God is the only thing that is real — and you are that! You are the extension of God's love, and luckily there is nothing you can do to alter that fact.

Exercise

What do you feel when you hear that you are an extension of the love of God? Say these words several times and see if anything shifts or changes in your body or mind:

"I AM the extension of the love of God."

Now shorten the phrase and see if the feeling increases or decreases:

"I AM the love of God."

Finally, shorten the phrase to the simplest form and say these words several times:

"I AM God."

Does it feel strange to make such a declaration? Until now you may have believed that such a statement was blasphemy. Perhaps your religious upbringing taught you that saying these words required severe punishment. But now you are coming into the true recognition of your Oneness with God, so declaring that this is what you are — an extension of the Divine in the world — should be natural and encouraged. Stay with this for a while until you feel the Truth radiating through your body and mind, then into the world as a blessing to all beings.

The Echo Chamber

There is nothing in this world that can contain you, so stop trying to retain, or hold onto, anything in this world. You still believe the container you call your identity defines the truth of who you are. It does not. It is like living in a tiny box thinking that the box you live in is the whole world. Your thoughts bounce off the inside of the box like an echo chamber, convincing you that what you are hearing is something other than your own voice. But now you are beginning to see an outline appear on the inside of the box, the outline of a door. You notice a bright light on the other side of the door; it is getting brighter every time you choose to listen to the Voice for God.

Touch the outline and see what happens. The door begins to open, even slightly, and you are able to see the inside of the box you have been living in for so long. You realize how small and constricted the box is, and you also see how big and amazing the world outside the box is. Step out and look around at the beauty that is all around you. Take a deep breath and fill your lungs with Heaven's fragrance.

Exercise

We used a similar analogy before, that of a tiny bird pecking away at the inside of a shell. Once the shell is broken you can never return. And the same is true when you break free into the Real World. The shell you called your identity has been destroyed and there is no reason for you to return.

Can you identify any of the ways you have felt this happening in your life? Has the shell begun to crack open letting you see the world in a new light? Perhaps you feel the desire to go back to your limited vision of yourself and the world. But is that even possible now? Decide to keep going, even if it is a little scary. As you emerge into the light, your eyes will adjust and you will be able to see in a way that was impossible before. Don't worry if it feels unusual or even scary. Just spread your new wings and feel yourself lifting off the ground.

It is time for you to fly.

The One

The moment you identify the one who *is*, the one who *is not* appears. This is the birthplace of every illusion. The instant you identify yourself (or another) as *the one*, you bring your entire focus to another who is *not the one*, and this is the beginning of all your troubles.

The One cannot be identified because then it is not *The One* but *one of many*, and separation reigns. Reality remains Real and Truth remains True despite your awareness of Reality or Truth, but your decision to deny this hides the Gift of God.

The One sees only The One, and that is how it knows itself as One. There is no *other*, no matter what appearances seem to reveal. The One who Knows they are The One sees through all appearances. They do not claim to be anything other than what they Truly are, and they give this gift freely and without exception. They look upon the sinner and the saint and see only Love. They look upon the servant and the King as the same reality expressed through a lens that has no lasting value. The only thing that lasts is Love, and ALL are contained within that Love since only Love is Real.

Exercise

Can you think of anyone who you put on a pedestal and said: "That person is enlightened and awake"? There is nothing wrong with recognizing a person who has fully embraced their wholeness. They can be an example for you to imitate and follow. But do you recognize them at the expense of someone you claim is not embracing their wholeness? In other words, is there anyone you think of and say, "That person is definitely not enlightened and awake"?

The focus of this lesson is to See everyone as God Sees them — as whole and awake regardless of how they act or behave. There have been many examples of people who claim to be enlightened but who were only trying to manipulate people into doing what they wanted them to do. Many people recognize their wholeness but have no need to draw attention to themselves. Once again, see if you can look at everyone in the same way — as perfect and whole, no matter what. If you are able to do this, even for a moment, then you will begin perceiving the same light within your own eyes.

God's Fool

The fool for God recognizes what they do not know, and that is why they possess the highest wisdom. A fool is humble, and that is why they see everything that exists, as opposed to that which could never exist.

There is a difference between being a fool for Heaven's sake and being foolish. A fool for God laughs at the foolishness of the world and in doing so rises above it. A foolish person (the one who considers him or herself wise in the ways of the world) constantly tries to move the pieces of perception around to create what they believe to be a better world, one that serves their own needs and desires. The fool for God never does this. They are too occupied with laughing at the laughable and loving that which is forever lovable.

If you want to be this kind of fool you will have to confront your need to be comfortable and right. A fool for God welcomes discomfort and realizes that they can not solve the problems of the world with the same problems that created the world. This one lets the impossible remain impossible and does not try to change anything. The fool for God exists beyond change in the changeless universe where love has no opposite, and being a fool for Heaven's sake is the highest wisdom.

Exercise

Are you willing to accept the foolishness that is described here? Does it embarrass you to act in a way that will confuse others or make you stand out as different? If so, then you may want to go back to the beginning of this book and start over. But if you are willing to do whatever it takes to awaken to the Real World, then laughing at the laughable will be easy.

See if you can act from this Divine foolishness today, in some small way. Even if you do it silently so no one else knows what you are doing, choose to see the world through this lens. Most of all, be willing to laugh at your own foolishness. You may find it profoundly liberating.

An Unwavering Desire

The world you see has absolutely nothing to do with who you are in the nondual universe, and anything that is not in the nondual universe is not real and can never represent who you truly are. This is the only thing you need to learn because it is the only thing that is True.

Every experience you have and every thought that comes into your mind either aligns with or conflicts with this Truth. And yet, since nothing that conflicts with this Truth is True, the experience you seek is simple to attain. All it takes is an unwavering desire to realize your wholeness and to know that you are wholly loved by a loving God. Every image of a vengeful God — which has nothing to do with your Creator but everything to do with your own need to condemn yourself — begins to fade just as the morning mist fades when sunlight penetrates the atmosphere. Every concept you hold about anything is replaced by the *original conception of grace*, unchangeable and undeniable, the holy extension of Love through which you were created and in which you remain.

This is all you need to break free from the illusions you have claimed until now. This is the only lesson you have yet to learn, and you will learn it as you choose to give everything to the One who is Everything.

Exercise

You may think that the play on words you read in this and many other lessons is simply that — a play on words. Since words are symbols of symbols this is the only real value words can actually have — to point you in the direction of Truth by manipulating the concepts that have manipulated you.

When you read: "Since nothing that conflicts with the Truth is True, the experience you seek is simple to attain," a lightbulb should go off within you that enables you to feel the reality behind the words or concepts. You will read many selections in this book that are aimed at breaking down the concepts in your mind using concepts that confuse the mind to reveal a deeper truth. Here is another example: "The One sees only The One, and that is how it knows itself as One." The intellectual mind becomes confused by such statements, creating an opening for wisdom to enter.

Your goal today is to welcome this intellectual confusion and notice what you feel within your heart. As always, these lessons are meant to encourage the journey from the mind to the heart, or from ideas to direct experience of the reality that lies beyond all ideas. See if you can access that reality today.

Are You Ready To Give Everything?

Give everything to know the One who is wholly present within and AS you now. Does this mean you should turn away from the world and give up your need to store up riches that are here today and gone tomorrow? Are you surprised when I tell you YES? Were you hoping there would be some kind of compromise, a loophole that would allow you to hold on to some aspects of the world but release what you choose to release?

All I will tell you is that the world you seem to see is not your real home, but there is another world beyond this one where you are completely at home. We call this the nondual universe. Now that you realize this you must do one of two things: accept what you hear and turn toward the Voice that speaks for love, or turn back like Lot's wife who couldn't give up what had already passed away. All I am telling you is that the world you think you see, the world where you cling to the hope that one day it will give you what you seek and want, is not real. But there is another world that will replace this one if you choose to See it. The choice or decision comes before the sight, so choose to See and a new world will appear before you. It really is that simple.

Exercise

As this lesson teaches, the decision to experience the Truth comes before you actually realize the Truth. Make that decision today. Decide that this is the ONLY thing you want to experience and it will be so. If you think you can pick and choose which parts of reality you want to embrace and which parts you want to reject, you will be lost in illusions. That is exactly what has happened before now. But you have come to a new point where you can make a total choice. A total choice is one where you are completely focused on one thing — seeing what is true. Don't try to keep some aspects of the dream because you think they are giving you something you need. Surrender it all and everything you truly need will be yours.

That Which Seems To Die

Facing your fear of an uncompromising spiritual commitment is the only thing left for you to accomplish. Why do you turn away from such a commitment? Somewhere within you, you know what you have always known, and that fact is frightening if you choose to hide from what you have always known. You have always known that love is your foundation and goal. You have always known that there is but one source of reality and that source is within you now. When you finally confront the denial of what you know to be true, what you know to be true will overtake you. When you feel the incredible freedom of an unqualified commitment to a single truth, you will laugh at the absurd self-constructed obstacles that have kept you from enlightenment. All you need to do to release these self-constructed obstacles is say these words and mean them with your whole heart:

"That which seems to die is not I. I AM
Awake Now!"

This is your freedom. This is the final and only step into your eternal reality. Claim that which has never stopped claiming you.

Exercise

Begin with this line from today's lesson:

"Somewhere within you, you know what you have always known, and that fact is frightening if you choose to hide from what you have always known."

If you have always known something but pretend to not know it, one of two things is true: you have either fallen asleep and have created a dream world where what you have always known is hidden from your sight, or you have willfully denied what you have always known. This is something ego has complete experience in — the willful denial of the Truth you have always known to be True. The Truth in you is perfect and whole this and every moment, but the split mind, also known as ego, refuses to believe this. It knows that its so-called reality is based on you believing that you are imperfect and broken, and it will use everything it can to maintain this belief.

Spend time today meditating on this line:

"I know what I have always known — I am perfect and whole at this moment."

Let these words wash over you and take the place of all the beliefs that have limited your ability to understand this simple truth.

All-Encompassing Love

You can only give to yourself. That fact will become more and more obvious as you give up trying to *give* or *get* anything from someone you believe to be outside yourself. And yet, even though you recognize this Truth intellectually you still believe you are in a reciprocal relationship with those who seem to *have* and those who *have not*. Trust Me when I tell you that no such distinction exists in reality. The *haves* are just as poor as the *have-nots* in this world, but you will refuse to realize that until you have a direct experience of the Love which IS all-encompassing.

So why not now? You still believe you will lose something you love if you accept the all-encompassing reality of Love. And then you wonder why a Whole-Mind points out this insanity and laughs at it. It is as if you have been standing on your head your entire life without realizing it. Everything you see is upside down, but you believe you are seeing it right side up. Then someone comes along who *does* see everything as it truly is and tries to explain your error to you. But since it seems impossible for you to accept that everything you have believed until now is the opposite of the Truth, you reject or even kill them. It is too threatening to realize that you have been looking at everything the wrong way and that nothing — literally nothing — you seem to see is real.

But here is the good news — Reality waits for you because Reality is timeless. It does not matter if it takes you three seconds to realize the Truth or three thousand lifetimes. The ending is inevitable since there never was a beginning.

Ah, now your mind begins to rattle. Read those words again:

The ending is inevitable since there never

was a true beginning.

This is the first thing you will realize when your mind finally flips and you are able to look at everything through the eyes of Love instead of the eyes of ego. You will finally realize the fact that dreams never really begin and never really end. Think about that for a moment. Even your nighttime dreams tell you this. You drop into a dream just like you dropped into this one. You are suddenly there, and when it is time to wake up you are suddenly not there. I promise you it is exactly the same when you wake up from ego's dream. The idea of a beginning and an end to the dream is in your mind, but not in the Mind of God. And if it is impossible for something to exist within the Mind of

God, then it is also impossible for it to exist in your mind.

Exercise

This lesson should fill you with a hint of nervousness as well as a great deal of relief. The feeling of nervousness comes from confronting the idea that you have been looking at everything, literally everything, upside down. In other words, you are seeing the world and everything in it as the opposite of how it Truly is. Your relief will come when you accept that you have now been offered a solution to the only problem you have ever had. Now that you accept that the split mind sees an impossible world, you can receive the gift of sight that your Whole-Mind reveals. This is the all-encompassing love described in this lesson, and it is finally an unshakable awareness that only increases as you move deeper into the Light.

Consider the possibility that the dream you are experiencing is similar to your nighttime dreams in the sense that it never had a true beginning and therefore never has a resolute end. Even if this is still a stretch, see if you can relax into this possibility. When you do you will be a step away from allowing the NOW that is always present to be your whole reality. And when you are able to rest fully in the NOW, the holy instant of your release will be at hand.

Everywhere At Every Moment

If you look for God *somewhere* you will never find God *everywhere*. You are looking for God *somewhere* because you think that you are *somewhere* — in a specific place at a specific time — and this could not be further from the truth. If you are one with God and God is everywhere at once, the same must apply to you. Period!

The Truth of You is everywhere at every moment, unlimited and eternal. Why would you seek anything less than this? Do you want to reduce yourself to less than the Truth of who you are in the Mind of God? This may sound strange but it is exactly what you have done. In your desire to prove yourself guilty for a sin you never actually committed you sought to reduce your reality to an illusory container you call a body with an inescapable end you call death. The idea that you return to a body again and again to repeat this cycle does not solve the problem. The only thing that will solve the problem you seem to have is to realize you have no problem at all because the problem you think you have is not shared by God. Any problem that is not in the mind of God can not be in your mind, but the illusion of the problem can indeed be in your mind, and this is your dilemma. You have mistaken an illusion of reality for reality itself, and you believe that you are bound by the inevitable result of this *mistake*. But God could never punish you for a mistake that had no true effect. If this were possible then God would not be loving, and love is the very essence of God.

You have created a God that punishes and condemns because you have punished and condemned yourself. But it is impossible for you to create God since the *created* cannot create the Creator. You are an extension of the Source of all Love, and there is nothing you can do to change this. You tried and you failed, and this is your greatest success. Embrace this failure and you will also be embracing the Truth of You that is forever held as True within the Mind of God. This is all you need to be saved from the ravishes of your split-mind. This is the only thing required to return your mind to the Wholeness that God loves.

Exercise

The possibility that the Truth of who you are — your soul — is everywhere at once, seems insane. Then again, everything you read in this book if you read it through the lens of the split mind, is insane. But the opposite will be true when your mind is fully healed. You will look back at all the strange beliefs that have captured your attention until now and see them for what they are — nothing. There will not be any judgment associated with this since judging something that is nothing is unreasonable. When your mind is finally healed of the split that seems to exist, keeping you from seeing what is so very clear to a Whole-Mind, you will simply laugh and move on. Joy will replace the confusion of seeing a world that could never possibly be real.

"If you look for God somewhere you will

never find God everywhere."

Let this be your goal today — to look for signs of Divinity everywhere you go, around every corner, and in the eyes of everyone you see. You will know you are successful at this when you feel a happiness that is beyond this world filling your heart. Do not hold back today. This could be the moment you break free from all the separating beliefs that have filled your mind until now into the open air where only love prevails.

Allow It To Be Done

The key to successful prayer is to *do* nothing, but allow it to be *done*. Trying to do anything is the admission that it is not true *now*. But everything true is always true, and Truth can only exist in the moment of now, which is the same as every moment because every moment IS now. This sounds like gibberish to the uncontrolled or split mind, but to a Whole-Mind, this is obvious and unquestionable. A Whole-Mind does not question anything but Sees Everything. What is not real is not seen, but what is forever real is unavoidable. Understand this and you will understand prayer.

You do not have the power to make anything real through effort or will. What is important here is God's Will, not yours. In God's Mind, every prayer has already been answered. In God's Mind, there can be no attack — only peace. So if you want to inspire peace in a given part of the world, accept it within yourself first. Choose to see what has always been Seen and everything else will align perfectly.

Exercise

This book is filled with lines like this one:

What is not real is not seen, but what is

forever real is unavoidable.

If you were able to fully comprehend any statement similar to this you could close this book and rest in the Truth. There would be nothing left for you to learn or gain because you would fully comprehend what seems so mysterious to the intellect but which is so clear to the soul. What is forever real is unavoidable because you can not live in a dream state forever where the rules of reality are reversed. You may be able to sleep for a very long time but you will ultimately reach the point where the dream becomes too chaotic to remain asleep. The only solution is to wake up and see where you are — safe at home.

Look at some of the things you claim as real but which never bring you the peace you desire. Perhaps you live in a place where peace is seldom known or experienced, and only conflict reigns. Do you believe you have the power to look through this conflict and see the peace that hides from your sight but which can be ignited by your choice to see only that? God's will is perfect peace, and if that is true then anything that seems to conflict with perfect peace is not real. Look through the illusion to what is real and what is real will be all you will see.

True Power

What the world calls power is the opposite of true power. The one who uses their strength to control or dominate others will themselves be dominated. The one who is humble will be lifted above the proud, and the one who surrenders to love will conquer the boastful. A country that relies upon the weapons of war to overwhelm a weaker country may seem to win the battle, but when the meek join together as one, all armies will be swept away.

My message is simple: do not become discouraged by the movement of weapons or the mobilization of armies. Their time is short in the Mind of God, but to the peacemaker, God will endow an eternal and everlasting reward.

Exercise

I have had the opportunity to travel and perform in many war zones and areas of great conflict and what I always find is the same: people like Me who are longing for the experience of peace. When I was with the Emissaries of Light in the mountains along the border of Croatia and Bosnia in 1995 I learned a chant that has remained with Me all these years: *Seek not peace here but find it everywhere.* In other words, do not look for peace in the world, or outside yourself, because you will never find it there. Look for peace within and it will suddenly show up everywhere. When I am in a country at war, my goal is not to solve a political issue that seems to have led to the conflict. My goal is to radiate peace and to invite others into that experience. When I do that then everyone I meet seems to match my experience. I could tell you many stories that illustrate this truth, and it is possible you could do the same.

See if you can remember a time in your own life when you felt great peace in a difficult environment. Perhaps there was conflict where you work among your co-workers. Did your decision to remain peaceful influence the others around you? Or maybe you were in the midst of the conflict, contributing to it in every way, then you made the decision to forgive or to see peace instead of the conflict. What effect did this have on the other people around you? Perhaps you found that the war dissolved before your eyes, or that the energy went out of the argument on its own. Let this be an example of today's lesson which says:

The one who is humble will be lifted above

the proud, and the one who surrenders to

love will conquer the boastful.

Everything

A bird can't explain to a fish what it feels like to fly, just as a fish can't describe what it feels like to swim to a bird. The only thing the bird needs to say to the fish is "jump," and the only thing the fish needs to say to the bird is "dive." If the fish decides to leap above the water's surface even for an instant, it will understand that the world is more than water, and if the bird decides to dive even a few inches beneath the waves, it will realize that the world is made of more than air. Both will experience that which the mind could never know and understand that which the intellect could never grasp.

Similarly a person whose mind has been made Whole cannot explain to a person whose mind is still split what it feels like to know God. A Whole-Mind simply points to the person's heart and says: "Everything!" If that person decides to rise above the current of their concepts they will See what has always been Seen, and Know what has always been Known. Then God will appear on its own.

Exercise

You can't use words to explain an experience that is wholly beyond words. But you can radiate an experience that words could never contain and in doing so, communicate something that lies beyond all concepts and words. St. Francis of Assisi once said: "Our only job is to preach the Gospel wherever we go and only when necessary, use words." He understood that it is easy to argue about words but the presence of peace is the greatest teacher in the world.

Find a way to share that presence today without using words. If you find yourself in a difficult situation hold still and radiate peace to everyone involved. Then watch as the people around you relax and the conflict dissolves. You may think that it is magic but what it is is the Truth taking hold of life.

A Single Goal

Your only goal now is to be perfectly certain that there is no alternative to the Will of God. Perfect Certainty! You may not yet realize that this is your only goal because many others still cloud your mind. But no other goal will bring you the joy Perfect Certainty brings, the goal which sets you free from the constraints of ego and the chains that bind you to illusions.

Until now you have chosen to *believe* that God's will can be opposed and that there is an alternative to the peace of God. Belief can be a helpful first step, but it will not set you free. Belief must shift into certainty, but this is not something you can force. It is a gift that is given to you when you decide that there is nothing left in this world to distract you from your single goal.

There is a tipping point where the goals of the perceptual world begin to dissolve and the discomfort you will feel when this happens cannot be underestimated. If you hold still within that discomfort and remain steady in your single desire, Perfect Certainty will prevail and you will begin to See everything anew. It will be like opening your eyes for the first time. What appeared dark and indistinct a moment ago comes into perfect focus, and once the Real World is truly known you will never be able to close your eyes again.

Exercise

The shift from faith or belief into Perfect Certainty has always been the goal of this course. It is impossible to describe how it will feel, but when the shift begins there will be no doubt. Perhaps you have already sensed its approach or felt the stir of this great ocean. Today's exercise is simple but it may be the final straw that helps you break free into the experience of certainty. Read the lesson again and say over and over as you read: "Yes." This signals to the Spirit within that you are ready and the experience of certainty will surely follow. When you say *yes*, see if you can feel an enormous weight being lifted off your shoulders, the weight of an entire world you created in your imagination. It is dissolving now, replaced by a world that is so light and so bright that you will wonder how you could have missed it before.

Eyes That See And Ears That Hear

You believe that what you hear is heard by all since you are completely convinced it is real. You think that what you see is seen by all since you are completely convinced that what you see is reality. But what if you learned that hearing what is true is not done with ears and seeing what is real is not done with eyes? Would you continue to rely upon the inconsistent evidence you use to prove the separating concepts you hold in your mind, or would you let them all go and choose to be guided into a new way of hearing and a new way of seeing? Begin here:

"I do not understand anything I see or

comprehend anything I hear."

Release every idea you have ever learned about this world and listen to the still, quiet voice that speaks to you when you are open and still. You may sense a Light beginning to grow inside you, a fire that builds as you surrender your vision to the One who knows how to interpret these symbols you call reality. Follow this Light and dive into this fire. Then your eyes will open and your ears will, at last, be unplugged. Then you will See that which has always

Seen you, and hear the Voice that calls to you this and every moment.

Until now you have chosen to walk through the world with your true eyes tightly closed, completely blocking out the Light. But now you have made a new choice — to part your eyelids the slightest degree, and in doing so, the Light pierces the darkness of your mind. Suddenly you see, though still dimly, what has always been Seen, and know what has always been Known. You have always been Seen, and You have always been Known. Now that you understand this, go out and share this gift with everyone you meet.

Exercise

Only when you close your eyes can you finally see the way. This makes no sense intellectually but it may help you understand what true sight offers and what your physical eyes will never reveal. Close your eyes right now and tune into the feeling of peace that rests at the center of your being. Even if it is only a murmur you can barely sense, give it your full attention. As you do, you will feel it begin to grow and replace the need to interpret everything you see through the lens of separation. There is a whole universe within you that is waiting to be revealed. It has been waiting for so long and yet this is the moment you finally awaken to its call.

The State Of Perfect Non-Being

You are being called into a state of Perfect non-Being which until now you have interpreted as death or loss. Perfect non-Being is actually the dissolving of the separate-self and the rising, or resurrection, of your Sacred Self. When the Sacred Self rises it is transformed and is no longer bound by the same laws that once seemed so insurmountable. This is the transcendent reality we share, regardless of whether you being aware or unaware of what is real.

To realize the state of Perfect non-Being simply relax and Be present to the Presence of I AM. A river flows without effort toward the ocean just as you flow effortlessly toward the ocean of Infinite Being. If you surrender to the current you will realize that though the quality of the river and the ocean differ (the ocean has salt while the river is clear of salt) they are actually connected and one. You will also realize that when the river reaches the ocean the river's current is no longer required. What is the purpose of the river's current? It is to draw you to the ocean. Once you arrive, your Being expands to include not only the river but every river that empties into the ocean. It is this emptying that is important. Let the current take you, then empty yourself of every longing and desire except to be one with this Infinite Ocean of Grace. Think of nothing but this, then you will dissolve and know that the river and the ocean are one.

Exercise

See if you can feel the current within pulling you into the ocean of Perfect Non-Being. You have become so distracted by the world you see with your eyes that you barely notice this river flowing within you. You cling to a branch or a tree at the river's edge and pretend that this is where you belong instead of the infinite ocean that calls for your return. Yes, you are being called home yet you pretend that you do not recognize the Voice that calls to you. Make the decision to hear today and follow the sound of that inner Voice. Close your eyes right now and see if you can hear what can never be heard with human ears, and feel what can never be felt by human hands. And when you do hear the call and feel the touch of grace upon your soul, don't turn back toward the world that has never given you what you truly desire. Move forward into the Light that illumines the Real World that is your true home.

The Solution Of The Soul

Your Soul, beyond all time and space, longs for nothing since it looks upon everything that is real and claims it as its own. It is secure within this reality and radiates the same, just as the sun is secure within itself and radiates its light, witnessing the birth of planets and galaxies. Now you are giving birth to the Holy Instant we share, and because we share it, it increases for all. What seemed to retract now expands, and since this sacred expansion has no end, it extends forever and forever.

Your identity, or who you believe yourself to be, constantly longs for more of what it does not have because it is insecure within its own unreality. It gathers and it claims, but nothing assures it of its safety. That is because it is never safe within the world it created to hide from reality. It finds security in being hidden, but now the Light has come and you can hide no more. Step out of the shadows, Holy Perfect Child of God, and see the Heaven that has been reserved for you before time began.

Exercise

We share the Holy Instant of NOW and that is why it increases without losing its essence and expands without losing its potency. Today we are going to attempt to feel and to know this increase by giving it away to as many people as we can. If possible, spend one hour giving the gift of wholeness to whoever you see. If you are walking, look at each person who passes you and SEE them for who they are — the holy extension of love's radiance. KNOW that they are One with you and with every Being that lives. If you are driving to work give the same gift to as many people as you can as they drive or walk past. If you do you will begin to feel a presence building inside of you. This presence is the Holy Instant itself. The more you choose to SEE what is true — the radiance that is assured to each ONE — the more you will feel the heat of this vibrant sun. The more you give the gift that has so freely been given to you the brighter the Light will become in your own soul.

So do not hesitate this day. You have said that this is the only thing you really, really want. Prove your devotion by giving it to everyone. Then you will be as God in the world since this is all God does — give wholly of Itself.

Understanding Level Confusion

What seems to go amiss on one level of experience does not affect all levels of experience, and yet this is what the split mind would have you believe. That is because the split mind, or ego, is forever confused about who you undeniably are.

An imbalance or a difficulty in the body does not interrupt or alter the perfection of the Soul. Why? Because the body is a temporary vehicle while the Soul is a permanent reality. All temporary vehicles change, age and ultimately decay. But the Soul does not change, it does not age and it cannot decay.

You may claim that you are not a body, and that would be true, but if you try to demonstrate this truth by stepping in front of a speeding bus, the body will be no more. However, the Soul — or the Truth of who you are — is not affected by this decision. You may claim that you are not a body, and once again, that would be true, but if this claim leads you to stop feeding the body, the body will cease to be, just as a car would cease to move if you deprived it of gasoline.

Jesus addressed this when he told us to "give unto Caesar what belongs to Caesar but give unto God what belongs to God". The Soul, or your unalterable, unchangeable reality, is who you are, and that reality belongs to God. If this is true then the body does not belong to God because it is changeable. Since the reality of God is unchangeable it stands to reason that the same applies to you because you are one with God.

So give unto the body what the body needs just as you would do to any vehicle, but don't confuse it with who you are in reality. Your soul needs nothing, but you would do well to give it your undivided attention, just as it always gives its undivided attention to you.

Exercise

You are not the identity you have claimed until now — a person who has a body, who is a certain age, and who lives in a certain city or town. None of these things describe who you REALLY are, the Self that is known by God. You are the single extension of holiness and light extending from the wholeness of your Creator. Does this surprise you? What about all the other people you see? Don't they deserve the same gift?

The idea that there are people who are cut off from the essence of your I AM reality is a construct of ego that needs to be separate from the inseparable. You see the bodies of other people walking through the world and immediately assume that they are unique in their reality. Uniqueness is the same as separation in this context. It is the same as focusing on the specialness of one person over another, believing that it makes them unique. Uniqueness and specialness exist only in ego's universe, but not the soul's.

You are here to focus all of your attention on the ONE who is revealed equally through every person you encounter. As you have read many times already, you are here to be as God in this and every moment — to See as God Sees, to Love as God Loves, and to Know what God Knows. See if you can sense this today through each person you see or pass. Be willing to lay aside their need to separate by laying aside your own.

You Returning To You

The split within your mind makes the simple seem difficult and the difficult seem simple. There is a simple answer to all your problems — the problems you think you have have already been solved. Can it be more simple than that? If you allow it to be so simple — and I assure you it is — you would immediately flash into Light and the world you think you see would completely vanish.

The split mind is determined to make you believe that it is possible to achieve the impossible. It is impossible for you to leave the Mind of God, yet you continue to assert that you have. You do this by leaving your Self — or projecting your unhealed judgments onto other people so you won't see how simple it is to undo all judgments. Once again, realizing how simple this can be achieved is the only thing you lack at this point. Accept this and you are Home.

If you decided to watch your mind and count the number of times you leave your Self to project your unhealed judgments onto other people, you would be shocked. It is so natural to the split mind that you don't even notice when you do it. Judgments begin in the mind and are then spoken by the tongue. This is how you justify the existence of the world you think you see.

What would happen if you reversed this habit and begin building one that leads to your release instead of your bondage? Begin by noticing when you speak about another person, in either a positive or negative manner, then return to your Self by stopping whatever conversation you are having. Pick a word to say that will signal your mind that you are making a new choice — a word like "Return." This tells your split mind that you are aware of its trick and refuse to play its game. Even if you practice this fifty or one hundred and fifty times in a given day, you will feel power beginning to grow inside you. This is You returning to You, and it is meant to lift your mind toward Heaven, but only if you give yourself wholly to the practice.

As this energy begins to build within you, you will be ready to take the next step. Now that you have become practiced in stopping the judgments from being spoken, you can begin watching the source of the projected judgments and stopping them before they even reach your tongue. Whenever you think a separating thought about another person, say the chosen word that leads you back to You. If your word is "Return," say or think it, then release the thought.

This will be very difficult in the beginning because you have become so proficient in projecting judgmental thoughts onto others, all for the purpose of keeping your mind distracted from your own holiness and perfection. Once again, as you become consistent in doing this, the power growing inside you will increase to the point that you will no longer be able to maintain your split-awareness of self. Then your Self will reign and you will begin to See what is always Seen by God, and you will Know what God has always Known.

Exercise

This lesson gives you everything you need to practice today. Simply decide to do what is being asked. You will likely notice a part of your mind that says something like: "Okay, I can do that," but if you do not make a serious effort to follow through, this will continue to be a theory but not an experience. Once again, give yourself to this practice today and every day. Pick a word that will signal your mind to return to a natural state of grace. Then use that word, even if you find yourself saying it hundreds of times every hour. This is mind training. You need to break the habits that have become so natural, replacing them with the habits that lead to your awareness of God.

The Illusion Of "i"

The illusion of "i" overwhelms the reality of I AM, but only when the mind attaches to any aspect of the world of form. When you detach from the world — step by step, moment by moment — forms begin to dissolve and fade, and you enter into a formless space where love is not opposed. Opposition to unified love is impossible in reality, but very possible in perception. That is because perception relies upon projection, and projection is always a choice.

You can choose to See as God Sees, or to see what is not Seen by God. You can also choose between projecting from the illusion of "i" or the reality of I AM, and the world you perceive will align with that choice. Now that you know what you are sacrificing by denying that which love (God) never denies, why would you make such a choice? Choose love because it is the only thing that exists in reality. It is a simple choice when perceived so simply.

Exercise

When you think of ego-mind in terms of a small "i" and your Whole-Mind as "I AM," the goal becomes clear. Why would you choose something so insignificant when you can choose the eternal I AM that is the essence of your Divine Nature? Once you realize that you have a choice it becomes simple and easy.

Until now you did not realize such a choice existed. You were born into a body, into a particular family who lives in a particular city or town. You had no choice in any of these things. It is impossible for you to realize that none of these things define what we are seeking to realize now. Everything described here may seem to be true, but what we are seeking is an experience that lies past this limited-truth. It is not the conditions of the body or personality we are concerned with here, but the eternal conditions of the soul.

Spend at least a half hour today examining all your past associations and asking: "Is this who I really am, this collection of experiences and beliefs?" Then see if you can touch something deeper, your essence that has nothing to do with the conditions of the body and personality. Make a resolute choice to feed this

Self with the only nourishment it needs — extending love to all. Then do what is required to keep this energy flowing by being the source of what you most desire.

The Key Attachment Of The Split-Mind

The key attachment of the split mind is the false concept of "i" with its history, ideas, and all its varied imaginings. Everything you see, when identified as separate or split from the I AM Presence you truly are, reinforces this attachment and builds an entire world to protect it. But the world you seem to have built to protect your attachments is not a real world but the projection of the false beliefs you hold about yourself. This is the "i" I AM is trying to get you to surrender. It is less than nothing because it is not seen or known by God. YOU are seen by God but you will not realize that until you choose to see your Self.

This is the most difficult thing you will ever be asked to accept, but accepting it is essential if you seek release from the key attachment of the split mind. It is an advanced realization, for sure, one that you are only now able to consider. Here it is: until now you were convinced that God cared about your life and your world. You were convinced that God loves the *you* you pretend to be. You imagined a benign Supreme Being that looks upon the world and either judges or blames what he sees. But the truth is — God does not even know you are here!

This is the greatest insult you can imagine. But before you react too strongly, consider this: do you love your child or anyone else for who they dream themselves to be, or do you love them for who they are when they wake up from their dream? Consider this again. Is it possible for you to truly know what your child is dreaming or who they think they are in that dream? Of course not! Your love goes to the one who sleeps, the child who will ultimately wake up and remember that they were never in any real danger, no matter what they beheld while they slept. The one God loves — which is who YOU are — is wholly protected from the dream of separation and death. But to realize this you must confront the false identity of "i." When you finally do this you will realize the true identity of "I AM."

The first step to being released from your attachment to this false concept of "i" is to stop protecting the world you created to hide from Reality. You protect what you love, and if you are protecting illusions that means you love them, or you value them more than Reality itself. Why would you do this unless you are confused about who you really are? All I am asking you to do is relax your clenched fists and let your arms rest comfortably at your side. You have been boxing with shadows for too long and the moment you give up the fight you will begin to See how simple salvation is.

Yes, salvation is simple indeed. The instant you choose to love that which is wholly lovable, you will awaken within the wholeness of that Love. Until then you will dream of an alternative to whole-love. Does it help for Me to tell you that no such alternative exists? Once again, no such alternative exists, so stop trying to prove the impossible. Just relax and let Me take you home!

Exercise

There is no alternative to love since love is not love unless it is whole. Ego has another concept of love, one that is unrecognizable to the soul. It believes in special-love instead of love that is given wholly and without reserve to all. This is really hate masquerading as love since its goal is to separate rather than unify.

See if it is possible to identify all the ways you have offered conditional love to others. If you are able to identify a person or a situation where this is true, simply choose again. There does not need to be any guilt associated with this choice, only the willingness to see past the decisions you made when you forgot that love is the only path that leads back to the reality you seek. See if it is possible to relax into that state of being today. If someone comes into your mind that you denied love to, decide again. Choose to see through the eyes of love that which is wholly lovable.

Liberation From Separate-Self

The activity of all living beings is to sustain Being-ness. Until realization of Self occurs, this is interpreted as sustaining or protecting the body and identity. Once liberation from the separate-self has been achieved, protecting the body and identity becomes a non-issue. The body will do what the body will do and the identity that seems to be separate from all other identities will begin to dissolve. This is what is known as freedom from self. Once again, until you fully release your body-identity this will seem like death, and so it shall be. But the instant you seek only the gifts of Heaven and deny the constraints of this world, you will realize the Truth that has always been True and the Reality that has always been Real.

Is this not what you really want? Unfortunately, the answer is no. You have wanted so many things and set your desire upon chains that bind rather than wings that fly. Why would you do this unless you are afraid of flying? Admit that you are content with chains because you still believe that you are guilty of a sin that never occurred in reality. Does it help to know that such a thing is impossible? Guilt belongs to the guilty and you are wholly innocent of sin. But you will not realize this until you offer the gift of guiltlessness to everyone you see or think of. Hold it back from anyone and you deny your Self. Why would you continue doing this when it has never given you what you really want? Only love can do this, and love will only come if you forgive everyone and everything, including and most especially yourself.

Exercise

It is time to offer forgiveness to the self that still believes in separation. When you are able to accomplish this, it will be easy to extend the same gift to others. But until now, offering forgiveness to the self you believe to be real felt like an impossible task. This is because you believe you will lose something you love by accepting everything that IS love. We have covered this before but it will serve us to look at it one last time.

You can't lose anything you love when you embrace everything that IS love. And since everything that IS real is contained within this love, everything is gained. Until now you have sought a partial gain rather than gaining EVERYTHING. Now you know what this has cost you and you can no longer continue the charade. Today's exercise, then, is to choose to stop accepting that which has never accepted you. If you can do this if even for an instant, the world will be filled with Light and you will finally see what your judgment has cost you. In that same instant, you will receive what love has always offered you.

Why Not Now?

You look at the world and what do you see? Can you find any consistency here? Can you find anything that remains the same forever? The world you perceive is the opposite of eternal and changeless, and the mind you use to see this unstable world sees changelessness as undesirable, even boring. Can you relate to this at all?

All I can tell you is that the Truth within you can never change, it never ends, and the experience of this Truth is anything but boring. It is up to you to look upon this or choose the illusions that seem to oppose Reality. You may choose to look upon the body that grows old and say: "this is real...this is who I am," but that does not make it so. You may choose to look upon the natural world and say: "this is the way of things...to die and decay," but that does not make it so.

There is an experience of Self that exists beyond the reach of all this. You are this Self, and this Self alone knows love. This Self alone is perfectly consistent in its thoughts, knows Its Creator, understands Itself, is perfect in Its knowledge and Its love, and never changes from Its constant state of union with Its Creator. This is who you are in Reality, and it is who you will always be.

So the choice you believe you have is really no choice at all. You will inevitably choose love because it is what you are in Truth, and you cannot claim what you are in illusions forever. Why not NOW?

Exercise

The question you read at the beginning and end of this lesson is critical to your awakening:

Why not NOW?

You may be able to finally realize that NOW is the only moment you can make this choice, so why put it off? Are you still afraid you will lose something if you claim Everything that is Real? Nothing is lost when you give up what has no value. Read that line again. *Nothing can be lost when you give up what has no value.* If you have not accepted the salvation this moment offers it means you are still not willing to give up the unreal and valueless. The instant you do this, stepping into the NOW will be easy and automatic. So once again, why not NOW?

The Moment You Have Been Waiting For

Your consciousness is the proof that God is. Without you, who is there to recognize God's greatness? You have been led to believe that there is a God outside of You who watches and judges your actions. But what if there is no God outside of You? If you truly are one with God and God is everywhere, then doesn't it stand to reason that you are everywhere as well? Even your logic proves that your reality cannot be challenged. Most of all, it cannot be challenged by the limited self you have claimed until now. Once again, if you are one with God and God is everywhere, in everything in every moment, isn't the same true of You?

This is the moment you have been waiting for. You have heard the Truth presented in a way that is difficult for your mind to reject. Will you accept the Truth that has always been True, or reject it as you have done many times before? I AM here to encourage you to stop rejecting that which has never rejected you. Reject nothing and you will realize how holy you are.

Exercise

Have you come to the point where it is difficult to deny the life you feel moving inside of you? A mother may deny she is pregnant as the unborn child grows within her, but when it begins to stir within her womb it becomes impossible to deny. The Truth is stirring within you now which means you are ready to step into the Light. This is the moment you have been waiting for, so step confidently into this new world. You will do so by affirming rather than denying the experience of your wholeness. The littleness you have claimed until now has never given you what you really want, so why continue to claim it? Why not let it dissolve into the Light where all dreams end and reality is seen for what it is — REAL!

See if you can tune in to the new life stirring inside you today. You may even feel it physically, and you will certainly feel its subtle growth if you try. Spend time cradling this new life, just as you would a newborn child, and let it increase until it is the only thing you know and the only thing you recognize.

There Is Nothing In This World That Can Contain You

A healed or a Whole Mind never looks for the solution to a problem within the world of form. A healed or a Whole Mind never even looks for the problem within the world. It is like searching for a rare gem in your dream, then waking up the instant you find it. Are you any richer for having found a priceless jewel while asleep and dreaming?

There is nothing in this world that can contain you, just as there is nothing in this world that will ever satisfy you. Seek and find what you will, but do not expect a true change to occur. You may set your mind on attracting the perfect mate, and you may accomplish the task. You may work for years to save enough money to buy the house of your dreams, but do not expect the house to ever leave your dream. Whatever is born within the dream stays within the dream, but that which lies beyond your imagined world remains unchanged forever. Most of all, you remain unchanged forever, perfect in your holiness. Seek only this realization and experience, then the dream forms that once attracted you will fade and dissolve, and all you will be left with is your Self.

Exercise

Are you finally ready? This is the final question to answer, and you are being asked to answer it even before you finish this course on the nondual universe. Are you finally ready to lay aside all the treasures you searched for and even found within the dream you chose instead of Heaven? Are you beginning to see how simple this is? Heaven is a choice you can make right now if you decide it is the only thing you want. But it needs to be the ONLY thing you want.

Until now you have wanted and hoped to claim so many things, and to a large degree, you have been successful. But your success has only led you deeper into the dream world, not released you from it. The more you accumulate and hold dear, the further you are from your real goal — the full experience of your wholeness. This is the same as describing your full return to the Heaven you never actually left.

You can return this very moment if you want. Nothing real has ever been lost so it should be simple to claim the Truth that is forever True. You will claim Heaven through your single desire to claim Heaven. Once again, this has to be the only thing you want. Spend time tuning in to that desire and see if you can amplify the feeling until it completely overwhelms every sound and image from the world of form. There is nothing in this world that can contain you unless you want to be contained. Break free NOW.

You Were Made For And By Love

Why spend so much time gazing at the picture of materialism that never satisfies or delivers on its promises? What has the material world ever promised that became a consistent reality? Your highest goal seems to be dying in the arms of someone you love or trying to insulate yourself from sickness, pain, and death by accumulating a long series of numbers in a bank account and the thin strips of paper those numbers seem to represent. Is this what you were made for?

No. This is not what you were made for. You were made for love alone since love alone created you perfect as Itself. Turn your gaze from what appears to be real to Reality itself. Only then will you feel the deep satisfaction you have lacked until now. This is the only thing you have lacked — the deep satisfaction of Knowing you are holy and whole. You could never lack wholeness just as you could never be separated from the holiness that rests at the very center of your being. The only thing you can lack is the knowledge or remembrance of this wholeness, but this is a choice you have made on your own. No one forced you to look away from that which is all-encompassing as if such a thing was possible. No one asked you to forget the One who could never forget you or could never stop loving you.

Turn your gaze from the *without* to the *within*, then the Kingdom of God will appear on its own.

Exercise

Recognizing your Creator will help you realize what you were created for. If your Creator, which is One with you Now, is the essence of Love, then it stands to reason that you were made by and for love. You will only come to know this through your consistent extension of the same — the Love that created and maintains your life.

Let this be a day for practicing one thing, the only thing that will help you realize the Oneness that can never be denied. You were literally created for this, and yet it is the one experience you are most afraid of — an all-encompassing love. You believe that something all-encompassing denies your reality in time, but the opposite is true. Rejecting this all-encompassing love has led to the collapse of your experience of love, but such a collapse cannot last forever. You are forever held within love whether you recognize it or not, so let this be a day for Seeing what has always been yours. As always, the surest way to accomplish this is to be the Source of that love for others.

God's Love Has Never Been Compromised

Everything begins and ends in the mind. The first thought that entered your mind when you were born is the same thought that will enter your mind when you leave your body — I AM. That is all you need to realize who you are, the Reality that God forever loves.

Neither the problem nor the solution is where you think they are. People will say: "This is where you should look," or "That is who we should blame." Do not listen to any of them. The problem and the solution are both in YOUR mind, nowhere else. Heal your mind and the world you perceive is automatically healed. Do not be alarmed by this. There is only ONE Mind and the idea that your individual mind is separate from ALL Mind is the only problem you have. It is only here, in this realization, that the only problem you have is already solved.

Others may call you insensitive and disconnected. They will say that you do not care about what is happening in the world, but you will respond by saying:

"I care TOTALLY, and that is how I Know I AM."

This is not a riddle for you to figure out in your mind, but a reality to be embraced by your soul. Embrace it now and you will realize that you never left your home and that God's love has never been compromised.

Exercise

How will you act when you achieve the full recognition of your wholeness? That is an impossible question to answer except to say that you will act however love directs you to act. Will you assert yourself into a situation that seems conflicted? If love directs this action then you will assert yourself. Will you work to heal the environment where you live, or do the work of reversing climate change? If love directs this action then you will follow. And yet, however love directs you there will be one thing you will always proclaim:

"Love cannot be changed or altered by what I do, but rather through who I AM."

Remember this always and you will be used as an instrument of peace in every moment.

You have an opportunity today to claim what has always claimed you — the love that is your very foundation. Seek to be the Source of this love and you will always be in the right place performing every task love requires. There is nothing for you to plan on your own, and no assertion of your individual will is needed. Simply follow the path laid out by love in every moment, then you will know who it is that acts through and as you.

There Is Nothing Left To Say

There never was anything to say other than *YES, I AM Here*. Anything else is a reduction. Anything more is impossible. God, or the essence of love itself, is calling you into an intimate experience and expression of NOW. Nothing has ever been said, or could ever be said, that will change this. God is calling you to THIS moment, and in this moment you have a choice. Will you affirm that which has always affirmed you? Or will you continue to deny that which could never deny you? This is the essence of your freedom, your freedom of choice. But you cannot choose what has never been real. You can create the illusion of choosing what could never be, but this is not a real choice. The only real choice is love because love is the only thing that is real.

Exercise

This lesson is a reaffirmation of every lesson in this course. You have the freedom to pretend to make Reality unreal, but you do not have the power to change Reality itself. You can make believe that you are vulnerable and weak, but that does not change the fact you are powerful beyond your imagining. All power lies within your mind, yet you have been too afraid to recognize and use your power to amplify love. All power lies within God's Mind, which means it is also in your mind. Until now you have chosen to use this power to see what could never be seen, but that has changed now. Now you See through new eyes and they reveal the world as it is — in Truth — shining in the radiance of Heaven.

This is the moment of choice. Will you affirm that which has always affirmed you? Say the words at the beginning of this lesson out loud in answer.

"Yes, I AM Here."

Say this throughout the day and watch as the world changes before your eyes. This is the moment you chose to awaken to the Love that has always been yours. Whenever you say these words feel the Light within increase and grow, then let it shine for all to see.

You Can Not Hide Forever

You have created in your own reflective associations a world that has no reality, but you are convinced that it does so you continue to deny who you are by living within the reflection instead of what is being reflected. Living in the reflection means you have disassociated from who you are, thinking you can hide in the mirror. But you can not hide there forever.

You have heard it said that God created the world because the only way God could know Itself was by creating something that seemed to be the opposite of Everything. You should know by now that there is nothing opposite to Everything, though this is what ego continues to assert. It is the same as saying you can not know what goodness is unless you experience the opposite of goodness, or you can not know that you are happy unless you experience being sad. This is one of the craziest ideas you have ever designed to justify what has no justification — that God somehow created the opposite of God in order to know God. You think it makes sense and that is the reason you still find yourself here. Let go of that one idea and you will pop into Heaven instantly, but you do not want to do that because it requires you to give up the idea of *two*. You are very comfortable with the concept of *two* but very frightened of the reality of *one*.

Your determination to see what isn't there has convinced you that *nothing* can exist. You look at a shadow and claim that it is real, and as long as you do, you will not realize that a shadow is nothing more than the manifestation of blocked light, which is exactly what your self-identity is. Until now you have been afraid to look at this, but a sufficient amount of light has come into your mind for you to see what has always been Seen by God. What has always been Seen by God is the only thing that is real — and you are that!

Exercise

Trying to create the opposite of Everything is impossible and insane. Yet your self-identity asserts that you can accomplish this, and it has tried over and over without success. When will you finally give up this vain attempt and surrender to Everything Real? You are real and forever will remain. Create whatever illusion you want or makeup whatever story you choose but it will not change this fact. Today's exercise is to stop trying to change the Will of God which is your salvation. It is time to receive the gift of a whole-reality which is all that exists. You can feel the dream coming to an end, so don't resist being guided into the Light. You have come so far, so step in with confidence and let grace lead you Home.

The Moment Of Your Awakening

Be very clear: This is the moment of your awakening. How do I know? Because this is the only moment that exists! How can I say that with such certainty? Because it is the only truth that has ever been expressed. The experience of your awakening to wholeness can only occur right NOW.

If you want to know this yourself then you must accept the means to receive it, and those means are before you this instant. They have always been before you but you are only now choosing to open your eyes to See them. If you accept this you will experience happiness beyond anything you have ever known before now. Why? Simply because this world you have claimed as your home has never delivered the happiness it promised. It gave the illusion of happiness, but what you are being offered now is no illusion. It is the only Truth that has ever existed in this make-believe world — your awakening to the experience of wholeness which has never been compromised!

It is never over until it is over and all I am telling you is that this was over a very long time ago. It was also over a second ago because there is no difference between a very long time ago and a second ago. They are both happening right now. You may separate them in your mind but that does not change what they are. You are being offered the experience of your awakening and there is only one possible result once this experience has been claimed — the recognition of what has always been true.

Exercise

You have come to the point where our exercises shift from *doing* to *being*. Does it help to know that you have done everything you need to do to reach your goal? All that is required now is to deepen your experience which is not something you do but something you allow to be done. That is the key, to allow everything real to be complete within you. I promise that this has already happened. There is no real alternative to this experience since the experience of Reality is the only thing that is Real. Spend time today relaxing into this and it will relax within you. This is all that is required now, relaxing into the Truth that has always been True.

God's Point Of View

All time is going on all of the time, but your need to draw time out into what appears to be *a long time* is the only thing that keeps you here. There is no such thing as *a long amount of time* because that would mean that there is also *a short amount of time.* There is no difference in the Mind of God, and that means there is no difference at all.

A long amount of time would have to be better than a short amount of time, or the other way around, depending on your point of view. It is your thinking you need to have a point of view that keeps getting you into trouble. Give up needing to have a specific point of view and you will realize all points of view in the same instant. That is all I am trying to teach and it is the only thing you need to learn — give up your limited point of view and enter into God's unlimited point of view.

God sees All in All. God's point of view is everywhere at the same time, yet it is also focused on the smallest atom or the tiniest grain of sand. How is it possible for both to be true? The whole universe is contained within the smallest atom and the tiniest grain of sand, and it is also contained within you.

Those who have eyes to see will see, and the moment you choose to open your spiritual eyes will be the same moment you realize that you have always been Seen by God.

Exercise

Until now you have chosen to limit your point of view to the tiniest possible space. Do you remember the analogy of the bird pecking at the inside of its shell trying to escape? What if you found yourself locked inside a shell but instead of breaking free you choose to remain there? The inside of the shell becomes a projection screen onto which you project all your ideas of the world you cannot see. You imagine what it will be like to break free from the shell but you never do what's required. Does this make sense to you now?

These lessons are like one tapping on the outside of the shell saying "It is time to break free." Will you listen and play your role, or will you choose to remain hidden? This is the moment you can decide to experience the Real World outside the shell where you have been hiding. All you need to do is realize that all the dreams you projected onto the inside of the shell were never real, then start breaking the shell that contains you. It will only take a moment, so why not begin now?

The Cornerstone Of God's Creation

Don't tell me what you think. I don't care what you think. Tell Me who you are — who you *really* are — and I will listen intently. Don't insist I give you the credit you think you deserve. A shadow deserves no credit at all, while total credit goes to the one who sees a shadow for what it is, then turns back toward the light. Don't spend your time telling me what you have learned. I am more interested in what you have unlearned and what you are willing to release.

You will never get into the Kingdom weighed down by concepts and beliefs. They are like full packs filled with rocks. Just run toward the gate and you will find it has always been open to you.

You are the very cornerstone of God's creation. Upon you has God's Holy Temple been built and it cannot fail since there is nothing created by God that could weaken or threaten the Kingdom. That would mean there must be a weakness within the Mind of God, and such a thing is impossible. If there is no weakness within God's Mind then it follows that there is none in yours because you share One Mind. If you would trust this fact then you would finally see the Vision of Holiness that has been reserved for you since the beginning of what you call time.

Exercise

Only ego declares who it is, what it has learned, and the value it believes it possesses and deserves. That is because ego is arrogant and believes that it is valuable on its own terms. But as the lesson describes, a shadow deserves no credit because it is not a real thing, just the manifestation of blocked light. Your identity is exactly the same and the quicker you turn toward the Light, the sooner you will recognize who you really are instead of who ego claims you to be.

When you read that the Truth in you is the actual cornerstone of God's creation, what do you feel? If you listen to ego's voice it will take full credit for this, but the soul remains quiet since it recognizes that the statement is not meant to prop up its own value. It is meant to give value to Everything created perfect and whole, which is another way of describing the Truth in you and everyone.

Look around yourself today and give this gift to the people you see or even think of. Their value is total but it is not intended for the personality which is in constant competition with everyone it sees. The cornerstone of God's creation is the whole Sonship, which is another way of describing the totality of God's love. You are contained within that wholeness,

just as everyone is contained since God's love is total
in every given moment.

The World You Seem To See

The degree to which your split mind asserts its identity to deny the Truth is unequaled in time and space. What you call time and space is precisely the assertion of your identity, and without that assertion, time in space would no longer exist. You want to portion out time and space according to your belief in your *self* instead of proclaiming that time and space are illusions meant to keep you from experiencing your eternal, whole nature. In other words, the *you* that you seem to be claiming is as unreal as the time and space you seem to inhabit, and if you would gladly accept that you would wake up in Heaven.

Instead, you point at the rosebush in the garden and say "maybe my ego isn't real but that rose certainly is." You actually have no idea what a rose is, so how can it be real? What you call a rose is nothing but an agreement you have made with other split minds to see something that isn't there. Wouldn't it be better to be uncompromising with what you are hearing right now? The world you seem to see is not real! Period. Come up with as many rosebush exceptions as you want but it will not change the Truth I AM pointing to.

Exercise

Are you willing to consider that the assertion of your identity is what makes time and space meaningful? This lesson is meant to be uncompromising with the Truth since your ego is uncompromising only with illusions. If you examine this you will realize that such a thing is impossible. You can not be uncompromising with something that does not exist. Admitting this fact will be the first step away from what has no value and toward an experience that has total value. As always, the choice is yours.

Today's exercise is simple: stop asserting your identity! You probably already know how difficult this will be since trying to stop asserting your identity is in itself an assertion of your identity! You can begin by holding still and asking for guidance and help. Remember, you can not do this on your own but there is One who is here to guide you. Open yourself to the still, quiet voice today and follow what you hear. It will never lead you astray.

Which Would You Choose: A Shield Or A Sword?

You are called to examine the Truth with uncompromising eyes and you have been given remarkable wisdom-tools to accomplish this — teachers and teachings, sacred texts, and holy gospels. Reach for the shield and you block the radiant light, all the while claiming to be Truth's disciple. Or you can reach for the sword and cut the security cord you have tied around yourself to keep you from falling too deep into this ocean of grace. The choice is yours, so once again, which will you choose?

Exercise

You may be asking yourself where this security cord is so you can begin cutting. It may shock you to realize that it is your need to keep your feet firmly planted in the world of duality, though you have been unable to recognize that until now. Cut the cord and you discover that you have always had wings to fly. Release the weight that keeps you bound to the limitations of form and the formless nondual universe will claim you as its own.

The Uncomfortable Path To God

Why are you seeking the comfortable path to God? Does it surprise you to hear that it does not exist? Why are you searching for lessons or books or teachers that make you feel good about where you are? You would be better off seeking a teacher who pushes you to see that you have no idea where you are, then challenges you to dive into the discomfort rather than avoid it. Stop moving from book to book or from one teacher to the next hoping to find the one who will tell you what you want to hear. Look for the one that tells you what you refuse to hear, the one that forces you to stretch further than you have ever stretched before. It may feel like your muscles are being torn apart when in reality you are like a tiny bird pecking away at the inside of a stubborn shell until it finally breaks open. Then you emerge into the light.

Exercise

Maybe you thought the last lessons in this program would tell you that you are on the right path. If you feel the sensation of fire lifting you above this world into the timeless reality of the nondual universe, then you are definitely on the right path. But if you are feeling comfortable with this new awareness, as if you have everything you need and your life will be smooth sailing from here, you might want to go back and reread some of these lessons. The ones that make you feel uncomfortable are likely the ones that have the most to teach you.

There is a saying originally expressed by Finley Peter Dunne in 1902 that reads: "Our role is to afflict the comfortable and comfort the afflicted." Perhaps those are God's words to anyone who uses spiritual principles to feel comfortable in the world. The world you see is not your real home and has never given you what you really, really want. So why look for salvation here when it can be easily found where it has always been — within you? See the Truth where it is this and every day, and be sure you offer it to everyone you meet, not so much through the words you speak but the love you share with all. That is the only exercise you need — be the Source of that which your soul longs for.

In Conclusion

This book and these lessons were never meant to speak to your mind, but to coax your soul into the experience of Reality which has always been Real. This is the only thing that matters — the experience of who you are and forever will remain. You will never understand these lessons intellectually. They are a slap in the face to your intellectual mind. Perhaps you felt it asserting itself and everything it believes as you read these lessons. But here is the thing to realize and realize with great joy:

You made it to the end!

You could have easily closed this book when the first lesson asserted:

"The Real cannot die; the unreal has never lived.

What I AM has always existed and remains

forever as it is and always will be."

But you kept reading, and you felt a fire growing within you as you did. Now you must continue to feed that fire. If you set this book aside but don't consistently affirm these lessons, the gravitational pull of ego will draw you back into the belief system it is most comfortable with — that you are guilty, vulnerable, and deserve punishment for all your sins. Listen instead to the Voice for God that says:

"You are innocent, invulnerable, and

deserve only the love in which you were

created and remain for all eternity."

Why turn your back on this when it gives you everything you want?

There are no more words that need to be expressed and no more concepts that need to be shared. You have everything you need to step away from the dualistic world into the nondual universe that has always been yours. This is the moment you decided to step into the Light because this is the only moment that exists. Embrace it now, just as it has always embraced you.

About the Author

James F. Twyman is an Episcopal/Anglican priest and a Franciscan brother in The Community of Francis and Clare. He has written 19 books including the NY Times bestseller *The Moses Code*, has directed or produced seven feature films including the award-winning *Redwood Highway* and *Indigo*, and has recorded nearly 20 music CDs. Known internationally as The Peace Troubadour, James has traveled to countries at war to perform The Peace Concert for over 25 years. During many of these peace journeys, he called people from around the world to pray and meditate for peace during World Synchronized Meditations. In some cases, millions of people participated in these meditations. James is also the founder and spiritual leader of Namaste Village, a nondual interfaith community in Ajijic, Mexico. For more information on Namaste Village go to www.Namaste-Village.com.